BOOK OF PIE

BOOK OF PIE

13-Digit ISBN: 978-1-64643-023-9
10-Digit ISBN: 1-64643-023-9

This book may be ordered by mail from the publisher. Please include $5.99 for postage and handling.
Please support your local bookseller first!

Books published by Cider Mill Press Book Publishers are available at special discounts for bulk purchases in the United States by corporations, institutions, and other organizations.
For more information, please contact the publisher.

Cider Mill Press Book Publishers
"Where good books are ready for press"
501 Nelson Place
Nashville, Tennessee 37214

cidermillpress.com

Typography: Adobe Garamond Pro, Black Jack, Gotham, and Type Embellishments One
Image credits: Pages 78, 108, 171, 175, 180, and 209 courtesy of Cider Mill Press Book Publishers.
All other images used under official license from Shutterstock and StockFood.
Cover image: Apple & Cranberry Pie, see page 104
Back cover image: Pecan Pie, see page 142
Front endpaper image: Linzer Pie, see page 126
Back endpaper image: All-American Apple Pie, see page 98

Printed in Malaysia

24 25 26 27 COS 8 7 6 5

BOOK OF PIE

Over 100 Recipes, from Savory Fillings to Flaky Crusts

CIDER MILL PRESS
BOOK PUBLISHERS

TABLE *of* CONTENTS

INTRODUCTION

❋ ❋ ❋

"Anytime is a good time for pie."

When Maria de Medeiros's Fabienne offered this response after Bruce Willis's Butch questioned her choice of blueberry pie for breakfast in the 1994 film *Pulp Fiction*, it was easy to imagine millions nodding along.

Simply put, pie, though frequently grouped behind other beloved treats like cake, cookies, and ice cream, has the most fervent devotees in the dessert game. As far as these folks are concerned, nothing else will do when the time comes for a treat. Dubious? Consider, for a minute, the apple pie's place as a stand-in for what is good about the American way of life—clearly, pie has transcended to a level few foods ever reach.

Cherry, blueberry, and strawberry rhubarb in the summer. Pumpkin during the holidays. Chocolate or banana cream at the diner after a late-night meal with a loved one. The presence of pie signals that something special is happening, and the warm memories we hold of our encounters with our favorites indicate that this communication comes through loud and clear.

In order to provide easier access to this exceptional realm, we provide the pie obsessive with information on everything from turning out a perfectly flaky crust to constructing those eye-popping confections you know from the diner. Within, you'll not only find the unparalleled comfort offered by the classics, there are savory pies, handpies, quiche—even one offering that stands as an homage to a cultural icon.

In other words, here's an entire book filled with answers to those prayers offered up by pie's true believers.

CHAPTER 1

CRUSTS

No matter how delicious the filling you've selected is, if your crust isn't up to snuff, your pie will fall far short of what you had in your head when you started out. Nothing is more fundamental to a great pie—and nothing easier to misfire on—than the crust.

To ensure that you always attain your mark, this chapter provides the keys to perfectly flaky piecrusts, as well as some fun alternatives that will help you put innovative twists on some of your favorite pies. There's also detailed breakdowns of key crust-related techniques like blind baking and crimping in order to provide your every preparation a solid foundation.

Perfect Piecrusts

YIELD: **2 PIECRUSTS**

ACTIVE TIME: **10 MINUTES**

TOTAL TIME: **2 HOURS AND 10 MINUTES**

INGREDIENTS

2½ CUPS ALL-PURPOSE FLOUR

1½ TABLESPOONS SUGAR

1 TEASPOON KOSHER SALT

¾ CUP LEAF LARD OR VEGETABLE SHORTENING

2 TABLESPOONS COLD UNSALTED BUTTER, DIVIDED INTO TABLESPOONS

5 TABLESPOONS ICE-COLD WATER, PLUS MORE AS NEEDED

DIRECTIONS

1. Place the flour, sugar, and salt in a bowl and stir until combined.
2. Add the lard or shortening and butter and use a pastry blender to work them into the flour mixture. Work the mixture until it is a coarse meal, making sure to break up any large chunks.
3. Add the water and continue to work the mixture until it is a smooth dough. If it feels too dry, incorporate more water in 1-teaspoon increments. Form the dough into a large ball and then cut it in half. Envelop each piece in plastic wrap and place in the refrigerator for 2 hours before using. The dough will keep in the refrigerator for up to 3 days. It also freezes very well, and can be stored in a freezer for up to 6 months.

BLIND BAKING

The technique of baking a piecrust before filling it is also known as "blind baking." When working with a custard filling, as in a lemon meringue or pumpkin pie, baking the crust ahead of time has several advantages. It prevents pockets of steam from forming in the crust once it is filled, which can cause the crust to become puffy and uneven. Blind baking also keeps the bottom of the crust from becoming soggy, and allows the edge of the pie to become sturdy. Uncooked rice is the most typical weight when blind baking a pie, though dried beans and weights designed specifically for the task can also be utilized. To blind bake a crust, place it in a 350°F oven and bake for 15 to 20 minutes, until it is golden brown and firm. Remove, dispense with the chosen weight, and let cool completely before filling the crust.

CRIMPING A PIECRUST

Crimping creates a decorative edge on your piecrust. It also defines it, keeping it from folding over in the oven. To crimp a piecrust, place your left thumb and left index finger approximately 1 inch from each other. Crook your right index finger and work your way around the pie plate, pressing your right index finger into that 1-inch space and against the inside edge of the piecrust.

Sweet Crusts

YIELD: **2 PIECRUSTS**

ACTIVE TIME: **10 MINUTES**

TOTAL TIME: **1 HOUR AND 10 MINUTES**

INGREDIENTS

2 STICKS UNSALTED BUTTER, AT ROOM TEMPERATURE

½ CUP SIFTED CONFECTIONERS' SUGAR

3 EGGS

¼ TEASPOON PURE VANILLA EXTRACT

2 CUPS ALL-PURPOSE FLOUR

½ TEASPOON BAKING POWDER

½ TEASPOON KOSHER SALT

DIRECTIONS

1. Place the butter in the mixing bowl of a stand mixer. Use the paddle attachment and beat on low until smooth. Add the sugar and beat at medium speed until smooth. Take care not to whip air into the mixture or the dough will become very hard to handle.

2. Add the eggs and vanilla and beat to incorporate, scraping down the mixing bowl as needed. Add the flour, baking powder, and salt and beat on low speed until the dough holds together. Divide the dough in two, envelop each piece in plastic wrap, and refrigerate for 1 hour before rolling out.

YIELD: **1 CRUST**

ACTIVE TIME: **20 MINUTES**

TOTAL TIME: **1 HOUR AND 15 MINUTES**

Cookie Crust

INGREDIENTS

2 STICKS UNSALTED BUTTER, AT ROOM TEMPERATURE

¾ CUP GENTLY PACKED LIGHT BROWN SUGAR

¾ CUP GRANULATED SUGAR

1 TABLESPOON PURE VANILLA EXTRACT

¾ CUP SEMISWEET CHOCOLATE CHIPS, MELTED

½ CUP UNSWEETENED COCOA POWDER

1 TEASPOON BAKING SODA

½ TEASPOON KOSHER SALT

1¾ CUPS ALL-PURPOSE FLOUR, PLUS MORE AS NEEDED

½ EGG WHITE

DIRECTIONS

1. Preheat the oven to 300°F and grease an 18 x 13-inch baking sheet with nonstick cooking spray. Place 1½ sticks of the butter and the sugars in a mixing bowl. Using a handheld mixer, beat the mixture until it is light and fluffy. Add the vanilla and melted chocolate and beat to combine, scraping down the mixing bowl as needed.

2. Sift the cocoa powder, baking soda, salt, and flour into a separate mixing bowl. Add the dry mixture to the wet mixture and stir until just combined. Place the dough on a flour-dusted work surface and roll it out so that it will fit the baking sheet and is approximately ⅛ inch thick.

3. Place in the oven and bake until firm, about 20 minutes. Check the crust after 15 minutes to make sure you don't overcook it—it is ready when you don't leave an impression while gently pressing down in the middle. Remove and let cool. While the crust is cooling, place the remaining butter in a saucepan and melt over medium-low heat. Leave the oven at 300°F.

4. Use a rolling pin or a food processor to break the crust up into crumbs. Place the crumbs in a mixing bowl, add the melted butter and egg white, and work the mixture with your hands until it becomes sticky.

5. Press the crumbs into a greased 9-inch pie plate and bake for 5 to 6 minutes, until the crust is firm. Remove from the oven and let cool before filling.

Cocoa Crust

YIELD: **1 PIECRUST**

ACTIVE TIME: **20 MINUTES**

TOTAL TIME: **2 HOURS**

INGREDIENTS

1 CUP ALL-PURPOSE FLOUR, PLUS MORE AS NEEDED

2 TABLESPOONS UNSWEETENED COCOA POWDER

2 TABLESPOONS SUGAR

½ TEASPOON KOSHER SALT

4 TABLESPOONS UNSALTED BUTTER

2 TABLESPOONS SHORTENING

1 LARGE EGG YOLK

2 TO 3 TABLESPOONS ICE-COLD WATER

DIRECTIONS

1. Place the flour, cocoa powder, sugar, and salt in a food processor and pulse until combined. Add the butter and shortening and pulse until the mixture resembles coarse crumbs. Add the egg yolk and water and pulse until the dough just holds together. Form the dough into a disk, envelop it in plastic wrap, and refrigerate for 1 hour.

2. Preheat the oven to 350°F. Remove the dough from the refrigerator and let it rest at room temperature for 5 to 10 minutes. Place the dough on a flour-dusted work surface and roll it out to ¼ inch thick. Place the crust in a greased 9-inch pie plate, line it with parchment paper, and fill it with uncooked rice. Place in the oven and bake for 15 to 20 minutes, until firm.

3. Remove from the oven, discard the rice and parchment paper, and let the crust cool completely before filling it.

YIELD: **1 PIECRUST**

ACTIVE TIME: **15 MINUTES**

TOTAL TIME: **1 HOUR AND 30 MINUTES**

Cornmeal Crust

INGREDIENTS

¾ CUP ALL-PURPOSE FLOUR, PLUS MORE AS NEEDED

¾ CUP CORNMEAL

½ TEASPOON KOSHER SALT

3 TABLESPOONS SUGAR (OPTIONAL)

1 STICK UNSALTED BUTTER, CHILLED AND CUT INTO SMALL PIECES, PLUS MORE AS NEEDED

1 EGG, LIGHTLY BEATEN

DIRECTIONS

1. In a large bowl, combine the flour, cornmeal, salt, and sugar (if using). Add the butter and work the mixture with a pastry blender until coarse crumbs form, making sure to break up any large chunks. Add the egg and work the mixture until the dough just holds together. Form the dough into a disk, envelop in plastic wrap, and refrigerate for 30 minutes.

2. Preheat the oven to 375°F. Remove the dough from the refrigerator and let it rest at room temperature for 5 to 10 minutes. Place the dough on a flour-dusted work surface and roll it out to ¼ inch thick. Place the crust in a greased 9-inch pie plate, line it with parchment paper, and fill it with uncooked rice. Place in the oven and bake for 12 minutes, until light brown and firm.

3. Remove from the oven, discard the rice and parchment paper, and let the crust cool completely before filling.

NOTE: Include the sugar if you are planning to use this crust to make a pie with a sweet filling.

YIELD: **1 SHELL**

ACTIVE TIME: **20 MINUTES**

TOTAL TIME: **2 HOURS AND 45 MINUTES**

Meringue Shell

INGREDIENTS

1 TABLESPOON UNSALTED BUTTER

3 EGG WHITES, AT ROOM TEMPERATURE

¼ TEASPOON CREAM OF TARTAR

¾ CUP SUGAR

½ TEASPOON PURE VANILLA EXTRACT

DIRECTIONS

1. Preheat the oven to 225°F and grease a 9-inch pie plate with the butter. Place the egg whites and cream of tartar in a mixing bowl. Using a handheld mixer, beat on high until foamy. With the mixer running, incorporate the sugar 2 tablespoons at a time, waiting until the sugar has dissolved before adding the next increment. Beat until the mixture is glossy and holds stiff peaks.

2. Add the vanilla, beat to incorporate, and spread the meringue over the pie plate, making sure to extend it all the way up the side. Place in the oven and bake for about 1 hour, until the meringue is firm and a toothpick inserted into the center comes out clean. Turn off the oven and allow the shell to rest in the cooling oven for 1 hour.

3. Remove from the oven, transfer the pie plate to a wire rack, and let cool completely before filling.

YIELD: **1 PIECRUST**

ACTIVE TIME: **10 MINUTES**

TOTAL TIME: **45 MINUTES**

Nutty Crust

INGREDIENTS

2 TABLESPOONS UNSALTED BUTTER, CHILLED AND CUT INTO SMALL PIECES, PLUS MORE AS NEEDED

1½ CUPS NUTS

1½ TABLESPOONS HONEY

DIRECTIONS

1. Preheat the oven to 400°F and generously grease a 9-inch pie plate with butter. Place the nuts in a food processor and pulse until you have a coarse meal.

2. Transfer the nuts to a bowl and add the honey and butter. Work the mixture with a pastry blender or your hands until combined. Press the mixture into the pie plate, place it in the oven, and bake for about 10 minutes, until the nuts look browned and smell toasted. Remove from the oven and let cool completely on a wire rack before filling.

   TIP: Any nut can be used to make this crust, but pecans and almonds produce the best results. Going with one of those and mixing in ¼ to ½ cup hazelnuts is another great option.

YIELD: **1 PIECRUST**

ACTIVE TIME: **10 MINUTES**

TOTAL TIME: **1 HOUR**

Graham Cracker Crust

INGREDIENTS

1½ CUPS GRAHAM CRACKER CRUMBS

2 TABLESPOONS SUGAR

1 TABLESPOON REAL MAPLE SYRUP

6 TABLESPOONS UNSALTED BUTTER, MELTED

DIRECTIONS

1. Preheat the oven to 375°F. Place the graham cracker crumbs and sugar in a large mixing bowl and stir to combine. Add the maple syrup and 5 tablespoons of the melted butter and stir until thoroughly combined.
2. Grease a 9-inch pie plate with the remaining butter. Pour the dough into the pie plate and gently press into shape. Line the crust with parchment paper, fill with uncooked rice, and bake for about 10 minutes, until the crust is firm.
3. Remove from the oven, discard the parchment paper and rice, and allow the crust to cool completely before filling.

YIELD: **1 PIECRUST**

ACTIVE TIME: **15 MINUTES**

TOTAL TIME: **1 HOUR**

Gluten-Free Crust

INGREDIENTS

1¼ CUPS GLUTEN-FREE FLOUR, PLUS MORE AS NEEDED

1 TABLESPOON SUGAR

½ TEASPOON XANTHAN GUM

½ TEASPOON KOSHER SALT

6 TABLESPOONS UNSALTED BUTTER, CHILLED AND CUT INTO SMALL PIECES

1 LARGE EGG

2 TEASPOONS FRESH LEMON JUICE

ICE-COLD WATER, AS NEEDED

DIRECTIONS

1. Place the flour, sugar, xanthan gum, and salt in a large mixing bowl. Add the butter and work the mixture with a pastry blender until a coarse meal forms.

2. Place the egg and lemon juice in a separate bowl and whisk briskly until the mixture is very foamy. Add it to the dry mixture and stir until the dough just holds together. If the dough isn't quite holding together, add the water in 1-tablespoon increments until it does. Form the dough into a disk, envelop it in plastic wrap, and refrigerate for 30 minutes.

3. Remove the dough from the refrigerator and let it rest at room temperature for 10 minutes. Place it on a flour-dusted work surface, roll it out to ¼ inch thick, and place it in a greased 9-inch pie plate.

CHAPTER 2

CREAM, CUSTARD & PUDDING

Remember your first encounter with one of these? How luscious it looked behind the glass in the dessert case at your favorite diner? How each bite exceeded those fantasies you'd conjured up?

Now you can bring that captivating quality right into your home. From classics such as chocolate cream (see page 31) and lemon meringue (see page 64) to surprising recipes like the Pear & Gingerbread Cream Pie (see page 60), you're sure to dazzle yourself, and anyone who happens past your table.

CHOCOLATE PUDDING

Place ¼ cup sugar, ½ cup sweetened cocoa powder, ¼ cup cornstarch, and ¾ teaspoon kosher salt in a saucepan, whisk to combine, and cook over medium heat. While whisking constantly, gradually incorporate 2½ cups whole milk. Cook until the mixture thickens and is close to coming to a boil. Reduce the heat to low and simmer for 1 to 2 minutes. Remove the saucepan from heat and stir in 6 tablespoons of unsalted butter and 2 teaspoons pure vanilla extract. Transfer the pudding to a bowl and place plastic wrap directly on the surface of the pudding to prevent a skin from forming. Place in the refrigerator for 2 hours before using.

YIELD: **8 SERVINGS**

ACTIVE TIME: **10 MINUTES**

TOTAL TIME: **3 HOURS AND 10 MINUTES**

Chocolate Cream Pie

INGREDIENTS

6 CUPS CHOCOLATE PUDDING (SEE SIDEBAR)

1 GRAHAM CRACKER CRUST (SEE PAGE 25)

2 CUPS WHIPPED CREAM (SEE PAGE 38)

CHOCOLATE SHAVINGS, RASPBERRIES, OR SLICED STRAWBERRIES, FOR GARNISH

DIRECTIONS

1. Put the pudding in the Graham Cracker Crust, smooth the top with a rubber spatula, and cover with plastic wrap. Refrigerate for 1 hour.

2. When ready to serve, place the Whipped Cream on top in a thick layer. Garnish with chocolate shavings, raspberries, or strawberries, if desired.

YIELD: **8 SERVINGS**

ACTIVE TIME: **15 MINUTES**

TOTAL TIME: **2 HOURS AND 15 MINUTES**

Chocolate Truffle Pie

INGREDIENTS

1½ CUPS HEAVY CREAM

2 CUPS BITTERSWEET CHOCOLATE CHIPS

4 TABLESPOONS UNSALTED BUTTER, DIVIDED INTO TABLESPOONS

2 TABLESPOONS CRÈME DE CACAO

1 COCOA CRUST (SEE PAGE 17)

DIRECTIONS

1. Preheat the oven to 350°F. Place the cream in a small saucepan and bring to a boil over medium heat. Place the chocolate chips in a heatproof bowl and then pour the boiling cream over the chocolate. Stir until the mixture is smooth, add the butter and liqueur, and stir to incorporate.

2. Place the filling in the crust, using a rubber spatula to distribute it evenly. Place in the refrigerator and chill for at least 2 hours before serving.

Chocolate Mousse Pie

YIELD: **8 SERVINGS**

ACTIVE TIME: **10 MINUTES**

TOTAL TIME: **2 HOURS AND 10 MINUTES**

INGREDIENTS

2 CUPS SEMISWEET CHOCOLATE CHIPS

2½ CUPS HEAVY CREAM

1 TABLESPOON BOURBON

1 TEASPOON PURE VANILLA EXTRACT

1 GRAHAM CRACKER CRUST (SEE PAGE 25)

DIRECTIONS

1. Preheat the oven to 350°F.
2. Place the chocolate chips in a microwave-safe bowl. Add ½ cup of the cream and stir. Microwave on medium, removing to stir every 15 seconds. When just melted, stir in the bourbon and vanilla and let the mixture stand for about 5 minutes.
3. In a large bowl, beat the remaining 2 cups of cream at medium-high speed with a handheld mixer until medium peaks form. Fold the chocolate mixture into the whipped cream. Pour the filling into the piecrust and smooth the top with a rubber spatula.
4. Place in the refrigerator and chill for at least 2 hours before serving.

YIELD: **8 SERVINGS**

ACTIVE TIME: **20 MINUTES**

TOTAL TIME: **2 HOURS AND 30 MINUTES**

Lemony Rice Pudding Pie

INGREDIENTS

3 CUPS LEMON CURD (SEE SIDEBAR)

2 CUPS WHOLE MILK

1 TEASPOON PURE VANILLA EXTRACT

1½ CUPS COOKED BROWN RICE

1 GRAHAM CRACKER CRUST (SEE PAGE 25)

1 CUP WHIPPED CREAM (SEE PAGE 38)

CINNAMON, FOR GARNISH (OPTIONAL)

DIRECTIONS

1. Place the Lemon Curd and milk in a large mixing bowl and whisk to combine. Add the vanilla and cooked rice and stir to combine.

2. Evenly distribute the filling in the piecrust, smoothing the top with a rubber spatula. Cover the pie with plastic wrap and place in the refrigerator for 2 hours.

3. Preheat the broiler on your oven. Remove the pie from the refrigerator and place it underneath the broiler. Broil until the top starts to brown, about 5 minutes. Remove and top each slice with Whipped Cream and, if desired, cinnamon.

LEMON CURD

Place 2 cups fresh lemon juice, 3 tablespoons lemon zest, 9 large eggs, 2 cups sugar, and 3 sticks of unsalted butter in the mixing bowl of a stand mixer fitted with the paddle attachment. Beat on medium speed until well combined. Pour the mixture into a saucepan and cook over low heat until it is thick enough to coat the back of a spoon, about 10 minutes. Pour the lemon curd into a serving dish, place in the refrigerator, and chill until it thickens further.

WHIPPED CREAM

Place 2 cups heavy cream and 1 teaspoon pure vanilla extract in a mixing bowl and whisk until soft peaks begin to form. Be sure not to overwork the mixture, as this will result in butter. Store in the refrigerator until ready to use.

YIELD: **8 SERVINGS**

ACTIVE TIME: **15 MINUTES**

TOTAL TIME: **1 HOUR**

Classic Key Lime Pie

INGREDIENTS

2 CUPS HEAVY CREAM

¼ CUP SUGAR

⅓ CUP FRESH KEY LIME JUICE

1 TABLESPOON GELATIN

½ CUP SWEETENED CONDENSED MILK

1 GRAHAM CRACKER CRUST (SEE PAGE 25)

WHIPPED CREAM (SEE SIDEBAR), FOR GARNISH

KEY LIME ZEST, FOR GARNISH

DIRECTIONS

1. Place the cream in a mixing bowl and beat until soft peaks start to form. Add the sugar and beat until stiff peaks start to form.

2. Place the key lime juice and gelatin in a small saucepan and stir until the gelatin has dissolved. Cook over medium heat until the mixture starts to thicken, about 3 to 5 minutes. Remove the pan from heat and allow to cool slightly. Stir in the condensed milk and then fold this mixture into the whipped cream resulting from Step 1.

3. Pour the filling into the crust, cover the pie with plastic wrap, and place in the refrigerator. Chill until set, about 45 minutes. Garnish with the Whipped Cream and key lime zest.

YIELD: **8 SERVINGS**

ACTIVE TIME: **30 MINUTES**

TOTAL TIME: **2 HOURS AND 30 MINUTES**

Banana Cream Pie

INGREDIENTS

1 CUP WHOLE MILK

1 CUP HEAVY CREAM

2 LARGE, VERY RIPE BANANAS, SLICED THIN

3 TABLESPOONS CORNSTARCH

3 EGG YOLKS

⅓ CUP REAL MAPLE SYRUP

1 TEASPOON PURE VANILLA EXTRACT

PINCH OF KOSHER SALT

1 GRAHAM CRACKER CRUST (SEE PAGE 25)

1½ CUPS WHIPPED CREAM (SEE PAGE 38)

DIRECTIONS

1. Place the milk and heavy cream in a saucepan and cook, stirring constantly, over medium heat until steam starts to rise off the mixture. Add the banana slices, reduce the heat to low, and use a fork to mash the fruit. Continue to cook over low heat, stirring occasionally, until the mixture is hot but not boiling. Incorporate the cornstarch 1 tablespoon at a time.

2. Beat the egg yolks until scrambled. Add the maple syrup and whisk to combine. While whisking constantly, add a ladleful of the hot milk mixture to the egg yolk mixture and whisk briskly to combine. Do this until you've incorporated about ½ cup of the milk mixture into the yolk mixture.

3. Whisk the tempered eggs into the mixture in the saucepan. Bring the mixture to a gentle simmer while stirring constantly. Remove from heat and stir in the vanilla and salt. Let the mixture cool completely.

4. Pour the filling into piecrust and refrigerate for 2 hours. Remove from the refrigerator, top with the Whipped Cream, and serve.

YIELD: **8 SERVINGS**

ACTIVE TIME: **15 MINUTES**

TOTAL TIME: **1 HOUR AND 15 MINUTES**

Banoffee Pie

INGREDIENTS

2 CUPS WHOLE MILK

1 TABLESPOON UNSALTED BUTTER

½ CUP SUGAR

3 TABLESPOONS CORNSTARCH

2 LARGE EGGS

PINCH OF KOSHER SALT

½ TEASPOON PURE VANILLA EXTRACT

2 LARGE BANANAS, SLICED

1 PERFECT PIECRUST, BLIND BAKED (SEE PAGES 10–11)

WHIPPED CREAM (SEE PAGE 38), AS NEEDED

DARK CHOCOLATE, SHAVED, FOR GARNISH

DIRECTIONS

1. Place the milk and butter in a saucepan and bring to a simmer over medium heat. As the mixture is coming to a simmer, place the sugar and cornstarch in a small bowl and whisk to combine. Add 2 large eggs and whisk until the mixture is smooth and creamy. While stirring constantly, gradually incorporate half of the milk mixture into the egg mixture.

2. Add the salt and vanilla to the egg mixture, stir to incorporate, and pour the tempered eggs into the saucepan. Cook, while stirring constantly, until the mixture is thick enough to coat the back of a wooden spoon, making sure not to let it come to a boil. Pour the custard into a bowl, place plastic wrap directly on the surface to prevent a skin from forming, and refrigerate until cool.

3. When the custard has cooled, place it in the bowl of a stand mixer fitted with the paddle attachment. Beat on low until smooth and creamy. Stir the banana slices into the custard and pour this mixture into the piecrust. Smooth the top with a rubber spatula.

4. Spread the Whipped Cream over the filling and sprinkle the chocolate shavings on top. Store in the refrigerator until ready to serve.

YIELD: **8 SERVINGS**

ACTIVE TIME: **15 MINUTES**

TOTAL TIME: **4 HOURS AND 30 MINUTES**

Raspberry Cream Pie

INGREDIENTS

2 CUPS CREAM CHEESE, AT ROOM TEMPERATURE

1⅔ CUPS SWEETENED CONDENSED MILK

1½ CUPS WHIPPED CREAM (SEE PAGE 38)

1 TEASPOON PURE VANILLA EXTRACT

1⅓ CUPS RASPBERRIES

1 COOKIE CRUST (SEE PAGE 14)

DIRECTIONS

1. Place the cream cheese in a mixing bowl and beat with a handheld mixer until smooth and creamy.
2. Stir in the condensed milk and then beat the mixture until it is smooth and thick. Fold in the Whipped Cream, vanilla, and raspberries.
3. Spoon the filling into the crust and use a rubber spatula to even out the top. Cover with plastic wrap and freeze until set, about 4 hours.
4. To serve, remove the pie from the freezer and let it rest at room temperature for 10 minutes before slicing.

YIELD: **8 SERVINGS**

ACTIVE TIME: **40 MINUTES**

TOTAL TIME: **6 HOURS**

Strawberry Cream Pie

INGREDIENTS

FOR THE PIE

1½ TABLESPOONS GELATIN

¼ CUP COLD WATER

1½ CUPS HULLED AND CHOPPED STRAWBERRIES

4 LARGE EGG YOLKS

⅔ CUP SUGAR

1 TABLESPOON FRESH LEMON JUICE

4 LARGE EGG WHITES, AT ROOM TEMPERATURE

¼ TEASPOON KOSHER SALT

1 GRAHAM CRACKER CRUST (SEE PAGE 25)

FOR THE TOPPING

1 TEASPOON GELATIN

2 TABLESPOONS COLD WATER

1 CUP HULLED STRAWBERRIES

1 TEASPOON FRESH LEMON JUICE

¼ CUP SUGAR

WHIPPED CREAM (SEE PAGE 38), AS NEEDED

2 OZ. BITTERSWEET CHOCOLATE, GRATED

DIRECTIONS

1. To begin preparations for the pie, combine the gelatin and water in a small bowl and let rest for 10 minutes.

2. Place the strawberries in a food processor and puree. Working over a heatproof bowl, strain the puree through a fine sieve to remove as many seeds as possible. Bring 1 inch of water to a simmer in a saucepan. Add the egg yolks, half of the sugar, and the lemon juice to the strawberry puree, stir to combine, and set the bowl over the saucepan. Cook, whisking constantly, until the mixture has thickened, about 5 minutes. Remove from heat and whisk in the gelatin slurry. Stir to combine and let the mixture cool for 10 minutes.

3. Place the egg whites and salt in a mixing bowl and whisk until frothy. Gradually whisk in the remaining sugar until the meringue holds soft peaks. Working in three increments, fold the meringue into the strawberry mixture. Spoon the mixture into the crust, cover, and chill for 4 hours.

4. To begin preparations for the topping, combine the gelatin and water in a small bowl and let the mixture rest for 10 minutes. Puree the strawberries with the lemon juice in a food processor. Strain the puree into a saucepan, add the sugar, and cook, while stirring, over medium heat until the mixture has thickened slightly, 3 to 5 minutes. Remove from heat and let cool.

5. Decorate the border of the pie with whipped cream, sprinkle the chocolate over the entire pie, and then spoon the strawberry syrup into the center. Refrigerate for another 30 minutes before serving.

YIELD: **8 SERVINGS**

ACTIVE TIME: **20 MINUTES**

TOTAL TIME: **4 HOURS AND 45 MINUTES**

Grasshopper Pie

INGREDIENTS

½ CUP WHOLE MILK

32 LARGE MARSHMALLOWS

¼ CUP GREEN CRÈME DE MENTHE

¼ CUP WHITE CRÈME DE CACAO

1½ CUPS WHIPPED CREAM (SEE PAGE 38)

1 TO 2 DROPS GREEN FOOD COLORING

1 COOKIE CRUST (SEE PAGE 14)

DIRECTIONS

1. Place the milk and the marshmallows in a large saucepan and cook over low heat, while stirring, until the marshmallows have melted. Place the pan in the refrigerator and chill for 20 minutes, stirring occasionally.

2. Stir the crème de menthe and the crème de cacao into the mixture. Fold the marshmallow mixture into the Whipped Cream and then incorporate the food coloring.

3. Place the filling in the crust, smoothing the top with a rubber spatula. Place in the refrigerator and chill for 4 hours before serving.

Irish Cream Pie

YIELD: **8 SERVINGS**

ACTIVE TIME: **15 MINUTES**

TOTAL TIME: **3 HOURS AND 30 MINUTES**

INGREDIENTS

2 CUPS WHITE CHOCOLATE CHIPS

⅓ CUP IRISH CREAM LIQUEUR

4 LARGE EGG WHITES

¼ CUP SUGAR

1 CUP HEAVY CREAM

1 GRAHAM CRACKER CRUST (SEE PAGE 25)

DIRECTIONS

1. Bring a half-full saucepan of water to a simmer. Place the white chocolate chips and liqueur in a heatproof bowl, place it over the simmering water, and let the mixture sit, stirring occasionally, until the chocolate has melted and the mixture is smooth. Remove from heat and let cool.

2. Place the egg whites in a separate bowl and beat with a handheld mixer until they can hold soft peaks. Incorporate the sugar 1 tablespoon at a time, and beat until the mixture holds stiff peaks.

3. Place the heavy cream in a separate mixing bowl, clean the beaters, and beat the cream until soft peaks form. Fold in the egg white mixture and the chocolate mixture. Distribute the mixture in the crust, cover with plastic wrap, and refrigerate for 3 hours before serving.

Caramel Cream Pie

YIELD: **8 SERVINGS**

ACTIVE TIME: **10 MINUTES**

TOTAL TIME: **45 MINUTES**

INGREDIENTS

1 CUP CREAM CHEESE, AT ROOM TEMPERATURE

⅔ CUP CHOCOLATE PUDDING (SEE PAGE 30 FOR HOMEMADE)

½ CUP WHOLE MILK

3 CUPS WHIPPED CREAM (SEE PAGE 38)

1 COCOA CRUST (SEE PAGE 17)

¼ CUP CARAMEL (SEE SIDEBAR)

1½ CUPS SHAVED CHOCOLATE

DIRECTIONS

1. Place the cream cheese in a mixing bowl and beat it with a handheld mixer until it is fluffy, about 2 minutes. Add the pudding and milk and beat until incorporated. Add 2 cups of the Whipped Cream and stir to combine. Spoon the mixture into the piecrust.

2. Drizzle 3 tablespoons of the Caramel on top of the mixture and use a knife to incorporate it in the filling. Cover with the remaining Whipped Cream and drizzle the remaining Caramel on top. Place in the freezer for 30 minutes.

3. Remove the pie from the freezer and sprinkle the chocolate over the top before serving.

CARAMEL

Place 1 cup sugar, ¼ cup water, 3 tablespoons unsalted butter, and ½ teaspoon kosher salt in a small saucepan and cook over medium-high heat until the mixture is light brown. Be sure not to stir the mixture; instead, gently swirl the pan a few times as it cooks. Reduce heat to medium and cook for about 3 to 5 minutes, or until the mixture caramelizes. Stir the mixture once or twice to make sure it does not burn. Remove from heat and let cool before using. This preparation will yield approximately 1 cup of caramel.

YIELD: **8 SERVINGS**

ACTIVE TIME: **25 MINUTES**

TOTAL TIME: **4 HOURS AND 30 MINUTES**

Mango Mousse Pie

INGREDIENTS

⅔ CUP UNSWEETENED SHREDDED COCONUT

1 PERFECT PIECRUST, BLIND BAKED (SEE PAGES 10–11)

1 TABLESPOON GELATIN

¼ CUP WATER

2 CUPS MANGO PUREE

⅔ CUP CASTER SUGAR

1¾ CUPS WHIPPED CREAM (SEE PAGE 38)

½ FRESH MANGO, PITTED, PEELED, AND SLICED THIN

1 SPRIG OF FRESH MINT

DIRECTIONS

1. Sprinkle the coconut over the blind-baked crust and set aside. Place the gelatin and water in a bowl and let the mixture rest for 5 minutes. Prepare an ice water bath in a large bowl or Dutch oven.

2. Place 1 cup of the mango puree and the sugar in a saucepan and cook over medium-low heat, stirring occasionally, until the sugar has dissolved. Add the gelatin slurry and stir until it has dissolved. Remove from heat and place the saucepan in the ice water bath. Add the remaining mango puree and stir until the mixture is cool to the touch.

3. Working in two increments, fold the mango mixture into the Whipped Cream. Pour the mousse into the crust, using a rubber spatula to smooth the top. Cover with plastic wrap and refrigerate for 4 hours.

4. To serve, top the pie with the slices of mango and the sprig of mint.

YIELD: **8 SERVINGS**

ACTIVE TIME: **20 MINUTES**

TOTAL TIME: **24 HOURS**

Poppy Seed Cream Pie

INGREDIENTS

½ CUP MILK

1¾ CUPS POPPY SEEDS

1 CUP GRANULATED SUGAR

2 TABLESPOONS UNSALTED BUTTER, MELTED

2 TABLESPOONS FRESH LEMON JUICE

1 PERFECT PIECRUST, BLIND BAKED (SEE PAGES 10–11)

1¼ CUPS CREAM CHEESE, AT ROOM TEMPERATURE

¼ CUP CONFECTIONERS' SUGAR

1 CUP SOUR CREAM, AT ROOM TEMPERATURE

⅔ CUP WHIPPED CREAM (SEE PAGE 38)

DIRECTIONS

1. Place a mixing bowl in the freezer. Place the milk in a small saucepan and warm over medium heat until steam starts to rise from the surface.

2. While the milk is warming, place the poppy seeds in a food processor and blitz until finely ground. Place them in a mixing bowl with ¾ cup of the granulated sugar, the butter, 1 tablespoon of the lemon juice, and the warmed milk. Stir to combine and spoon the filling into the crust, using a rubber spatula to smooth the top. Cover and place the pie in the refrigerator.

3. Place the cream cheese and remaining sugar in a mixing bowl and beat with a handheld mixer until fluffy. Add the confectioners' sugar, sour cream, and remaining lemon juice and beat until well combined. Working in three increments, fold the Whipped Cream into the mixture. Top the pie with the mixture, cover the pie with plastic wrap, and refrigerate overnight before serving.

Vanilla & Coconut Cream Pie

YIELD: **8 SERVINGS**

ACTIVE TIME: **30 MINUTES**

TOTAL TIME: **24 HOURS**

INGREDIENTS

1 CUP SWEETENED SHREDDED COCONUT

¾ CUP SUGAR

3 TABLESPOONS CORNSTARCH

¼ TEASPOON KOSHER SALT

2½ CUPS WHOLE MILK

½ CUP HEAVY CREAM

3 LARGE EGGS

1 TABLESPOON UNSALTED BUTTER

1 TABLESPOON PURE VANILLA EXTRACT

1 PERFECT PIECRUST, BLIND BAKED (SEE PAGES 10–11)

DIRECTIONS

1. Place the coconut in a large dry skillet and toast, stirring often, over medium heat until it is fragrant and golden brown, about 2 to 3 minutes. Transfer to a bowl and set aside.
2. Place the sugar, cornstarch, and salt in a saucepan and stir to combine. Whisk in the milk and cream and cook the mixture over medium heat until it has thickened and started to bubble, about 2 to 3 minutes. Remove from heat and set aside.
3. Place the eggs in a heatproof bowl and whisk until scrambled. Gradually whisk in about 1 cup of the hot milk mixture and then pour the tempered eggs into the pan. Cook, stirring constantly, over medium heat until the mixture is just about to come to a boil. Reduce the heat to low and continue stirring the mixture for another 2 minutes.
4. Remove from heat and whisk in the butter, vanilla, and toasted coconut. Pour the mixture into the piecrust, place it in the oven, and bake until it is set and golden brown on top, 25 to 30 minutes. Remove from the oven and transfer to a wire rack to cool completely. Cover with plastic wrap and refrigerate overnight before serving.

Pear & Gingerbread Cream Pie

YIELD: **8 SERVINGS**

ACTIVE TIME: **20 MINUTES**

TOTAL TIME: **2 HOURS**

INGREDIENTS

4 TABLESPOONS UNSALTED BUTTER, AT ROOM TEMPERATURE

½ CUP GENTLY PACKED LIGHT BROWN SUGAR

¼ CUP GRANULATED SUGAR

¼ CUP MOLASSES

3 TABLESPOONS ALL-PURPOSE FLOUR

¼ TEASPOON KOSHER SALT

1 TEASPOON GROUND GINGER

1 TEASPOON CINNAMON

⅛ TEASPOON ALLSPICE

⅛ TEASPOON GRATED FRESH NUTMEG

3 LARGE EGGS

1 CUP HEAVY CREAM

1 TEASPOON PURE VANILLA EXTRACT

1 PERFECT PIECRUST, BLIND BAKED (SEE PAGES 10–11)

3 TO 4 PEARS, PEELED, CORED, AND HALVED

2 TABLESPOONS SLIVERED ALMONDS, LIGHTLY TOASTED

DIRECTIONS

1. Preheat the oven to 350°F. Place the butter and sugars in a mixing bowl and beat with a handheld mixer until pale and fluffy. Add the molasses, beat to incorporate, and then stir in the flour, salt, and spices.
2. Incorporate the eggs one at a time, scraping down the bowl as needed. Add the cream and vanilla, stir to incorporate, and pour the filling into the crust, making sure it is distributed evenly. Distribute the pear halves evenly atop the filling.
3. Place the pie in the oven and bake for 45 to 50 minutes, until the filling is set, browned, and puffy. Remove from the oven and let the pie cool completely. Sprinkle the slivered almonds on top and serve.

YIELD: **8 SERVINGS**

ACTIVE TIME: **25 MINUTES**

TOTAL TIME: **2 HOURS**

Sour Cream & Pear Pie

INGREDIENTS

1 PERFECT PIECRUST (SEE PAGE 10)

1¼ CUPS SOUR CREAM

¾ CUP GRANULATED SUGAR

¾ CUP ALL-PURPOSE FLOUR

¼ TEASPOON KOSHER SALT, PLUS A PINCH

2 TEASPOONS PURE VANILLA EXTRACT

1 EGG

5 CUPS PEELED AND SLICED PEARS

3 TABLESPOONS REAL MAPLE SYRUP

¼ CUP GENTLY PACKED LIGHT BROWN SUGAR

½ TEASPOON GROUND CARDAMOM

3 TABLESPOONS UNSALTED BUTTER, CHILLED AND CUT INTO SLIVERS

DIRECTIONS

1. Preheat the oven to 400°F. Grease a 9-inch pie plate with nonstick cooking spray and place the crust in it.

2. Place the sour cream, sugar, ¼ cup of the flour, the ¼ teaspoon salt, vanilla, and egg in a mixing bowl and whisk until combined. Stir in the pear slices and evenly distribute the mixture in the crust.

3. Place the remaining flour and salt, the maple syrup, brown sugar, and cardamom in a bowl and stir to combine. Add the butter and work the mixture with a pastry blender until coarse crumbs start to form. Place the mixture in the refrigerator.

4. Place the pie in the oven and bake for 15 minutes. Reduce the temperature to 350°F and bake for another 30 minutes. Remove the pie from the oven, take the butter-and-brown sugar mixture out of the refrigerator, and sprinkle it over the pie. Bake for another 20 to 25 minutes, until topping is golden brown. Remove from the oven and let the pie cool before serving.

YIELD: **8 SERVINGS**

ACTIVE TIME: **30 MINUTES**

TOTAL TIME: **1 HOUR AND 30 MINUTES**

Lemon Meringue Pie

INGREDIENTS

FOR THE PIE

¼ CUP CORNSTARCH

¼ CUP ALL-PURPOSE FLOUR

1¾ CUPS SUGAR

¼ TEASPOON KOSHER SALT

2 CUPS WATER

4 EGG YOLKS, LIGHTLY BEATEN

½ CUP FRESH LEMON JUICE

1½ TABLESPOONS LEMON ZEST

2 TABLESPOONS UNSALTED BUTTER

1 PERFECT PIECRUST, BLIND BAKED (SEE PAGES 10–11)

FOR THE MERINGUE

4 EGG WHITES

¼ TEASPOON CREAM OF TARTAR

PINCH OF KOSHER SALT

½ CUP SUGAR

1 TEASPOON FRESH LEMON JUICE

DIRECTIONS

1. To begin preparations for the pie, place the cornstarch, flour, sugar, and salt in a saucepan and stir until well combined. Add the water in a slow stream and stir until incorporated. Cook the mixture over medium heat, while stirring occasionally, until it is thick, about 20 minutes. Remove from heat.

2. While whisking constantly, add ¼ cup of the mixture in the saucepan to the beaten egg yolks. Stir the tempered eggs into the saucepan and place it over medium-low heat.

3. Add the lemon juice, lemon zest, and butter and stir constantly until the mixture is thick enough to coat the back of a wooden spoon. Remove the mixture from heat and let it cool completely. Preheat the oven to 400°F.

4. Add the cooled filling to the piecrust and use a rubber spatula to smooth the top.

5. To prepare the meringue, place the egg whites, cream of tartar, and salt in a mixing bowl and beat with a handheld mixer until stiff peaks start to form. Gradually add the sugar and beat until the sugar has dissolved and the mixture is very stiff. Gently fold in the lemon juice.

6. Spread the meringue over the filling and use a large spoon or a rubber spatula to create swirled peaks. Place in the oven and bake until the peaks of meringue are light brown, about 6 minutes. Remove from the oven and let the pie cool completely before serving.

Ginger & Key Lime Custard Pie

YIELD: **8 SERVINGS**

ACTIVE TIME: **20 MINUTES**

TOTAL TIME: **1 HOUR AND 30 MINUTES**

INGREDIENTS

FOR THE CRUST

8 TO 10 GINGERSNAP COOKIES

½-INCH PIECE OF FRESH GINGER, PEELED AND GRATED

1 STICK UNSALTED BUTTER, MELTED

FOR THE FILLING

1 (14 OZ.) CAN OF SWEETENED CONDENSED MILK

½ CUP FRESH KEY LIME JUICE

4 LARGE EGG YOLKS

1 TABLESPOON PURE VANILLA EXTRACT

FOR GARNISH

1 CUP WHIPPED CREAM (SEE PAGE 38)

1 TABLESPOON KEY LIME ZEST

DIRECTIONS

1. Preheat the oven to 350°F and grease a 9-inch pie plate with nonstick cooking spray.
2. To begin preparations for the crust, place the cookies in a food processor and blitz until they are crumbs. You can also put the cookies in a resealable plastic bag and use a rolling pin to grind them into crumbs.
3. Place the crumbs in a bowl, add the ginger and melted butter, and stir until the mixture is like wet sand. Press the mixture into the greased pie plate.
4. Place the crust in the oven and bake until it is firm, about 10 minutes. Remove from the oven and let cool. Reduce the oven's temperature to 325°F.
5. To prepare the filling, place the condensed milk, key lime juice, egg yolks, and vanilla in a bowl and mix until combined. Pour the filling into the cooled crust.
6. Place the pie in the oven and bake for about 20 to 30 minutes, until the filling has set into a soft custard. Remove from the oven and let cool completely before serving. Top each slice with Whipped Cream and a sprinkle of the key lime zest.

YIELD: **8 SERVINGS**

ACTIVE TIME: **40 MINUTES**

TOTAL TIME: **24 HOURS**

Mandarin Meringue Pie

INGREDIENTS

FOR THE PIE

2 LARGE EGGS

4 LARGE EGG YOLKS

¾ CUP CASTER SUGAR

1½ TABLESPOONS CORNSTARCH

¼ TEASPOON KOSHER SALT

1¼ CUPS FRESH MANDARIN ORANGE JUICE

⅓ CUP FRESH LEMON JUICE

1½ STICKS UNSALTED BUTTER, CHILLED AND DIVIDED INTO TEASPOONS

1 PERFECT PIECRUST, BLIND BAKED (SEE PAGES 10–11)

FOR THE MERINGUE

2 LARGE EGG WHITES, AT ROOM TEMPERATURE

PINCH OF KOSHER SALT

PINCH OF CREAM OF TARTAR

½ CUP SUGAR

¼ CUP WATER

FOR GARNISH

ZEST OF 2 MANDARIN ORANGES, CUT INTO STRIPS

DIRECTIONS

1. To begin preparations for the pie, place a few inches of water in a saucepan and bring to a simmer. Place the eggs, egg yolks, sugar, cornstarch, and salt in a large heatproof bowl and whisk until the mixture is light and fluffy. Gradually whisk in the orange juice and lemon juice.

2. Place the bowl over the simmering water and cook, stirring occasionally, until the mixture thickens, about 8 to 10 minutes. Remove from heat and stir in the butter 1 tablespoon at a time. Let the mixture cool for 15 minutes. Preheat the oven to 350°F.

3. Pour the mixture into the piecrust, place the pie in the oven, and bake for about 10 minutes, until the curd is just set. Remove the pie from the oven, let it cool completely on a wire rack, cover with plastic wrap, and chill overnight.

4. To prepare the meringue, place the egg whites, salt, and cream of tartar in a mixing bowl and beat until the mixture holds soft peaks. Place the sugar and water in a saucepan and cook over medium heat, stirring constantly, until the sugar has dissolved and the mixture comes to a boil. Cook for another 2 minutes and then gradually incorporate the syrup into the egg white mixture. Whisk until the meringue is thick, glossy, and cool to the touch. If desired, brown the meringue with a chef's torch or under the broiler. Garnish with the strips of zest and serve.

Strawberry & Coconut Meringue Pie

YIELD: **8 SERVINGS**

ACTIVE TIME: **25 MINUTES**

TOTAL TIME: **1 HOUR AND 30 MINUTES**

INGREDIENTS

FOR THE PIE

3 CUPS HULLED STRAWBERRIES

½ CUP SUGAR

1 TEASPOON FRESH LEMON JUICE

PINCH OF KOSHER SALT

2 TABLESPOONS CORNSTARCH

2 TABLESPOONS COCONUT RUM OR COCONUT MILK

1 PERFECT PIECRUST, BLIND BAKED (SEE PAGES 10–11)

FOR THE MERINGUE

3 LARGE EGG WHITES, AT ROOM TEMPERATURE

PINCH OF KOSHER SALT

¼ TEASPOON CREAM OF TARTAR

⅔ CUP SUGAR

⅓ CUP WATER

¾ CUP UNSWEETENED SHREDDED COCONUT

DIRECTIONS

1. To begin preparations for the pie, place 2½ cups of the strawberries in a saucepan and mash them. Stir in the sugar, lemon juice, and salt and cook over medium heat, stirring occasionally, until the mixture has thickened slightly, about 5 minutes.

2. Place the cornstarch and coconut rum (or coconut milk) in a small bowl and stir to combine. Stir this mixture into the strawberries and cook, stirring constantly, for 1 minute. Remove from heat and let the mixture cool.

3. To prepare the meringue, place the egg whites, salt, and cream of tartar in a mixing bowl and beat until the mixture holds soft peaks. Place the sugar and water in a saucepan and cook over medium heat, stirring constantly, until the sugar has dissolved and the mixture comes to a boil. Cook for another 2 minutes and then gradually incorporate the syrup into the egg white mixture. Whisk until the meringue is thick, glossy, and cool to the touch. Fold in ½ cup of the coconut.

4. Spoon the strawberry mixture into the piecrust and smooth the top with a rubber spatula. Spread the meringue over the filling and, if desired, brown it with a chef's torch or under the broiler. Sprinkle the remaining coconut and strawberries on top and serve.

Coconut Dream Pie

YIELD: **8 SERVINGS**

ACTIVE TIME: **15 MINUTES**

TOTAL TIME: **1 HOUR AND 30 MINUTES**

INGREDIENTS

1 (14 OZ.) CAN OF UNSWEETENED COCONUT MILK

1 CUP WHOLE MILK

¾ CUP UNSWEETENED SHREDDED COCONUT, LIGHTLY TOASTED, PLUS MORE AS NEEDED

10 TABLESPOONS SUGAR

3 EGGS

4½ TABLESPOONS CORNSTARCH

3 TABLESPOONS UNSALTED BUTTER

2 TEASPOONS PURE VANILLA EXTRACT

2 TEASPOONS PURE COCONUT EXTRACT

1 PERFECT PIECRUST, BLIND BAKED (SEE PAGES 10–11)

1½ CUPS WHIPPED CREAM (SEE PAGE 38)

DIRECTIONS

1. Place the coconut milk, milk, shredded coconut, and ½ cup of the sugar in a large saucepan and stir to combine. Bring to a simmer over medium heat.
2. While the mixture in the saucepan is warming, place the eggs, the remaining sugar, and the cornstarch in a mixing bowl and whisk until the mixture is smooth.
3. While whisking constantly, incorporate the mixture in the saucepan into the egg mixture in ½-cup increments. When you have incorporated 2 cups of the mixture in the saucepan, whisk the tempered eggs into the saucepan and cook, while stirring constantly, until the mixture is thick enough to coat the back of a wooden spoon. Remove from heat, add the butter, vanilla, and coconut extract, and stir to incorporate.
4. Fill the piecrust with the mixture, cover it with plastic wrap, and refrigerate until cool.
5. When the filling is cool, top with the Whipped Cream and additional coconut and serve.

Millionaires' Pie

YIELD: **8 SERVINGS**

ACTIVE TIME: **30 MINUTES**

TOTAL TIME: **5 HOURS AND 30 MINUTES**

INGREDIENTS

1 TABLESPOON GELATIN

¼ CUP COLD WATER

4 LARGE EGG YOLKS

⅔ CUP SUGAR

1 CUP CRUSHED PINEAPPLE, DRAINED

1 TABLESPOON FRESH LEMON JUICE

4 LARGE EGG WHITES, AT ROOM TEMPERATURE

¼ TEASPOON KOSHER SALT

1 GRAHAM CRACKER CRUST (SEE PAGE 25)

1½ CUPS WHIPPED CREAM, FOR TOPPING

DIRECTIONS

1. Place the gelatin and water in a small bowl and let the mixture rest for 10 minutes.

2. Place a few inches of water in a saucepan and bring to a simmer. Place the egg yolks, half of the sugar, the crushed pineapple, and lemon juice in a heatproof bowl and stir to combine. Place the bowl over the simmering water and cook, while stirring constantly, until the mixture has thickened, about 5 minutes. Remove from heat and stir the gelatin slurry into the mixture. Let the mixture cool for about 10 minutes. It should thicken as it cools.

3. Place the egg whites and salt in a mixing bowl and whisk until frothy. Gradually incorporate the remaining sugar and beat the mixture until it holds soft peaks. Working in three increments, fold the meringue into the pineapple mixture. Spoon the mixture into the piecrust, cover the pie with plastic wrap, and refrigerate for 4 hours.

4. Top the pie with the Whipped Cream, cover with plastic wrap, and refrigerate for another hour before serving.

TIP: To give the flavor of this pie a bump, add ⅓ cup of ground pecans to the mixture when making the piecrust.

Caramelized Peach Custard Pie

YIELD: **8 SERVINGS**

ACTIVE TIME: **25 MINUTES**

TOTAL TIME: **2 HOURS**

INGREDIENTS

2 TABLESPOONS UNSALTED BUTTER

2 LARGE PEACHES, PITTED AND SLICED

7 TABLESPOONS SUGAR

¼ TEASPOON CINNAMON

2 TABLESPOONS BRANDY

½ CUP WHOLE MILK

½ CUP HEAVY CREAM

2 EGGS

1 EGG YOLK

½ TEASPOON PURE VANILLA EXTRACT

¼ TEASPOON KOSHER SALT

1 PERFECT PIECRUST, BLIND BAKED (SEE PAGES 10–11)

DIRECTIONS

1. Place the butter in a skillet and melt over medium-high heat. Add the peaches to the melted butter and cook, turning the slices as they cook, until they are brown on all sides.
2. Sprinkle 3 tablespoons of the sugar and all of the cinnamon over the peaches and shake the pan until they are evenly coated. Cook until the peaches start to caramelize, about 8 minutes.
3. Tilt the pan away from you, add the brandy, and use a long match or wand lighter to ignite it. Shake the pan until the alcohol cooks off and then pour the mixture into a heatproof mixing bowl. Let the mixture cool.
4. Preheat the oven to 300°F. When the flambéed peaches are close to cool, place the milk, heavy cream, eggs, egg yolk, remaining sugar, vanilla, and salt in a mixing bowl and whisk to combine.
5. Evenly distribute the flambéed peaches in the piecrust and then strain the custard over the top. Place the tart in the oven and bake until the custard is just set, 20 to 25 minutes. Remove from the oven and let cool before serving.

Chocolate Meringue Pie

YIELD: **8 SERVINGS**

ACTIVE TIME: **25 MINUTES**

TOTAL TIME: **2 HOURS**

INGREDIENTS

FOR THE PIE

5 TABLESPOONS CAKE FLOUR

½ CUP SIFTED UNSWEETENED COCOA POWDER

⅛ TEASPOON KOSHER SALT

2¼ CUPS SUGAR

¾ CUP WATER

5 LARGE EGG YOLKS

1¾ CUPS EVAPORATED MILK

SEEDS OF 2½ VANILLA BEANS

2½ TABLESPOONS UNSALTED BUTTER, CUT INTO SMALL PIECES

1 PERFECT PIECRUST, BLIND BAKED (SEE PAGES 10–11)

FOR THE MERINGUE

1½ EGG WHITES, AT ROOM TEMPERATURE

½ TEASPOON CREAM OF TARTAR

1¼ CUPS SUGAR

DIRECTIONS

1. To begin preparations for the pie, place the flour, cocoa powder, salt, and sugar in a bowl and whisk to combine. Place the water and egg yolks in a separate bowl, whisk to combine, and then strain this mixture into the evaporated milk. Add the dry mixture and whisk to combine.

2. Place the mixture in a saucepan and bring to a boil over medium heat while stirring constantly. Remove from heat, add the vanilla seeds and butter, and beat with a handheld mixer until smooth. Cover the saucepan and set it aside.

3. Preheat the oven to 300°F. To prepare the meringue, place the egg whites and cream of tartar in the mixing bowl of a stand mixer and beat at high speed until frothy. With the mixer running, gradually incorporate the sugar and beat until stiff peaks form.

4. Pour the filling into the crust and top with the meringue. Place in the oven and bake until a few cracks form in the meringue, about 45 minutes. Remove from the oven and let cool before serving.

YIELD: **8 SERVINGS**

ACTIVE TIME: **15 MINUTES**

TOTAL TIME: **1 HOUR AND 30 MINUTES**

White Chocolate Pie

INGREDIENTS

¾ LB. WHITE CHOCOLATE CHIPS

1 STICK UNSALTED BUTTER, CUT INTO SMALL PIECES

2 EGGS

1 CUP HEAVY CREAM

½ CUP SUGAR

1 TEASPOON PURE VANILLA EXTRACT

PINCH OF KOSHER SALT

1 SWEET CRUST (SEE PAGE 13), BLIND BAKED (SEE PAGE 11)

WHITE CHOCOLATE, SHAVED, FOR GARNISH

¼ CUP HULLED AND SLICED STRAWBERRIES, FOR GARNISH

DIRECTIONS

1. Place the white chocolate chips and butter in a small saucepan and cook over low heat, stirring frequently, until melted and combined. Remove from heat and aside.

2. In a bowl, whisk together the eggs, cream, sugar, vanilla, and salt. Incorporate the white chocolate mixture and then whisk until thoroughly combined. Pour the filling into the crust and shake the pie plate to evenly distribute.

3. Place the pie in the oven and bake for 15 to 20 minutes, until the filling is set around the edges but still soft in the center. Remove from the oven and let cool completely before topping with the white chocolate shavings and strawberries.

WHITE CHOCOLATE

While some apocryphal tales assert that white chocolate is the result of cocoa beans that have not been roasted, that is far from the case. White chocolate is instead made with cocoa butter (a product resulting from roasted cocoa beans), sugar, and milk powder. As it does not contain the cocoa mass that is produced by grinding the roasted nibs of the cacao bean finely, some do not consider white chocolate to be a true chocolate.

Carrot & White Chocolate Pie

YIELD: **8 SERVINGS**

ACTIVE TIME: **20 MINUTES**

TOTAL TIME: **2 HOURS AND 15 MINUTES**

INGREDIENTS

6 CUPS PEELED AND CHOPPED CARROTS

4 TABLESPOONS UNSALTED BUTTER, DIVIDED INTO TABLESPOONS

2 TEASPOONS PURE VANILLA EXTRACT

¾ CUP FINELY CHOPPED WHITE CHOCOLATE

2 TEASPOONS GROUND GINGER

1 LARGE EGG

3 LARGE EGG YOLKS

1¼ CUPS GENTLY PACKED LIGHT BROWN SUGAR

1¼ CUPS SOUR CREAM

1 GRAHAM CRACKER CRUST (SEE PAGE 25)

DIRECTIONS

1. Preheat the oven to 400°F. Place the carrots, butter, and vanilla in a large mixing bowl and stir to combine. Place the mixture on a large, rimmed baking sheet and roast, removing to toss two or three times, for about 1 hour, until the carrots are fork-tender.

2. Remove from the oven and place the carrots in a food processor. Pulse until minced, add the white chocolate, and pulse until it has melted. Add the ground ginger, egg, egg yolks, light brown sugar, and sour cream and puree until smooth, scraping down the work bowl as needed. Reduce the oven's temperature to 325°F.

3. Evenly distribute the filling in the piecrust, place the pie in the oven, and bake for about 50 minutes, until the filling is set and dry to the touch. Remove from the oven and let cool before serving.

YIELD: **8 SERVINGS**

ACTIVE TIME: **15 MINUTES**

TOTAL TIME: **1 HOUR AND 30 MINUTES**

Pumpkin Pie

INGREDIENTS

1 (14 OZ.) CAN OF PUMPKIN PUREE

1 (12 OZ.) CAN OF EVAPORATED MILK

2 EGGS, LIGHTLY BEATEN

½ CUP GRANULATED SUGAR

½ TEASPOON KOSHER SALT

1 TEASPOON CINNAMON

¼ TEASPOON GROUND GINGER

¼ TEASPOON GROUND NUTMEG

1 PERFECT PIECRUST, BLIND BAKED (SEE PAGES 10–11)

DIRECTIONS

1. Preheat the oven to 400°F. In a large bowl, combine the pumpkin puree, evaporated milk, eggs, sugar, salt, cinnamon, ginger, and nutmeg. Stir until thoroughly combined.

2. Working with the crust in the pie plate, fill it with the pumpkin mixture. Smooth the surface with a rubber spatula.

3. Place the pie in the oven and bake for 15 minutes. Reduce the heat to 325°F and bake for an additional 30 to 45 minutes, until the filling is firm and a toothpick inserted in the middle comes out clean. Remove the pie from the oven and allow to cool before serving.

YIELD: **8 SERVINGS**

ACTIVE TIME: **15 MINUTES**

TOTAL TIME: **2 HOURS**

Spicy Pumpkin Pie

INGREDIENTS

⅔ CUP GENTLY PACKED DARK BROWN SUGAR

4 EGGS

1 (14 OZ.) CAN OF PUMPKIN PUREE

1 TEASPOON CINNAMON

1 TEASPOON GROUND GINGER

½ TEASPOON GRATED FRESH NUTMEG

¼ TEASPOON GROUND CLOVES

CAYENNE PEPPER, TO TASTE

2 TABLESPOONS SPICED RUM

¼ TEASPOON KOSHER SALT

1½ CUPS HEAVY CREAM

1 PERFECT PIECRUST, BLIND BAKED (SEE PAGES 10–11)

12 TO 14 GINGERSNAPS

DIRECTIONS

1. Preheat the oven to 375°F.

2. Place the sugar, eggs, and pumpkin in a mixing bowl and beat until the sugar begins to dissolve. Add the spices, rum, salt, and the cream and beat until incorporated.

3. Cover the bottom of the piecrust with the ginger snaps.

4. Place the pie in the oven and bake for 15 minutes. Reduce the heat to 325°F and bake for an additional 30 to 45 minutes, until the filling is firm and a toothpick inserted in the middle comes out clean. Remove the pie from the oven and allow to cool before serving.

YIELD: **8 SERVINGS**

ACTIVE TIME: **25 MINUTES**

TOTAL TIME: **2 HOURS**

Sweet Potato Pie

INGREDIENTS

2 CUPS COOKED AND MASHED SWEET POTATOES

1½ CUPS EVAPORATED MILK

2 EGGS, LIGHTLY BEATEN

½ CUP GRANULATED SUGAR

½ TEASPOON KOSHER SALT

1 TEASPOON CINNAMON

¼ TEASPOON GROUND GINGER

¼ TEASPOON GROUND NUTMEG

1 STICK UNSALTED BUTTER

1 CUP GENTLY PACKED LIGHT BROWN SUGAR

1 PERFECT PIECRUST (SEE PAGE 10)

DIRECTIONS

1. Preheat the oven to 400°F. Place the mashed sweet potatoes, evaporated milk, eggs, granulated sugar, salt, cinnamon, ginger, and nutmeg in a bowl and stir until combined.
2. Place a 10-inch cast-iron skillet over medium heat and melt the butter in it. Add the brown sugar and cook, while stirring constantly, until the sugar is dissolved. Remove the pan from heat.
3. Place the piecrust over the butter-and-brown sugar mixture in the skillet. Place the skillet in the oven and bake for 15 minutes.
4. Remove the skillet from the oven and briefly let the crust cool. Evenly distribute the sweet potato mixture in the crust. Place the pie in the oven and bake for 15 minutes.
5. Reduce the oven temperature to 325°F and bake until the filling is set and a toothpick inserted in its center comes out clean, about 30 minutes. Remove the skillet from the oven and let cool before serving.

Gluten-Free Grapefruit Custard Pie

YIELD: **8 SERVINGS**

ACTIVE TIME: **40 MINUTES**

TOTAL TIME: **5 HOURS**

INGREDIENTS

2½ CUPS SUGAR

½ CUP ALL-PURPOSE GLUTEN-FREE FLOUR

4 EGG YOLKS

4 RED GRAPEFRUITS, PEELED, PITH REMOVED, AND SECTIONS CUT IN HALF

2 CUPS WATER

2 CUPS SWEETENED CONDENSED MILK

1 TEASPOON PURE VANILLA EXTRACT

1 GLUTEN-FREE PIECRUST (SEE PAGE 26), BLIND BAKED (SEE PAGE 11)

WHIPPED CREAM (SEE PAGE 38), AS NEEDED

DIRECTIONS

1. Place 2 cups of the sugar and the flour in a bowl and stir to combine. Place the egg yolks in another bowl and whisk until frothy.

2. Place the grapefruit pieces in a saucepan and cover them with the water. Cook over medium-high heat, stirring constantly, until the water comes to a boil. Add the remaining sugar and continue to stir for another 10 minutes as the mixture boils. The grapefruit sections will fall apart and yield a thick, pulpy mixture.

3. Remove the saucepan from heat and stir in the sugar-and-flour mixture. Add the sweetened condensed milk and stir gently to combine. While whisking constantly, add a ladleful of the hot grapefruit mixture into the egg yolks. Incorporate another ladleful into the egg yolks and then stir the tempered egg yolks into the saucepan. Place over medium heat and cook, stirring constantly, for about 6 minutes, taking care that the mixture does not come to a boil. Remove from heat and stir in the vanilla.

4. Pour the mixture into the piecrust and use a rubber spatula to smooth the top. Cover with plastic wrap and refrigerate for 3 hours. To serve, top each slice of pie with some Whipped Cream.

YIELD: **8 SERVINGS**

ACTIVE TIME: **35 MINUTES**

TOTAL TIME: **24 HOURS**

Cranberry Curd Pie

INGREDIENTS

FOR THE PIE

3 CUPS CRANBERRIES

JUICE OF 1 ORANGE

1¼ CUPS SUGAR

2 LARGE EGGS

2 LARGE EGG YOLKS

1 STICK UNSALTED BUTTER, AT ROOM TEMPERATURE

1 TEASPOON PURE VANILLA EXTRACT

PINCH OF KOSHER SALT

1 PERFECT PIECRUST, BLIND BAKED (SEE PAGES 10–11)

FOR THE TOPPING

1 CUP HEAVY CREAM

¼ CUP SIFTED CONFECTIONERS' SUGAR

1 TEASPOON PURE VANILLA EXTRACT

½ CUP POMEGRANATE SEEDS

LEAVES FROM 3 SPRIGS OF FRESH THYME

DIRECTIONS

1. To begin preparations for the pie, place the cranberries and orange juice in a large saucepan and cook, stirring occasionally, over medium heat until the cranberries soften and split, about 10 to 15 minutes.

2. Strain the mixture through a fine sieve into a clean saucepan. Add the sugar, eggs, egg yolks, butter, vanilla, and salt and stir to combine. Cook over low heat, stirring frequently, until the curd thickens, about 10 minutes. Strain the curd into a mixing bowl and let cool slightly. Preheat the oven to 350°F.

3. Pour the curd into the crust, place the pie in the oven, and bake for 10 to 12 minutes, until the curd is just set. Remove from the oven, let cool completely on a wire rack, and refrigerate overnight.

4. To prepare the topping, place the cream, confectioners' sugar, and vanilla in a mixing bowl and beat until the mixture holds soft peaks. Spoon the whipped cream over the pie and top with the pomegranate seeds and thyme.

Buttermilk Pie

YIELD: **8 SERVINGS**

ACTIVE TIME: **10 MINUTES**

TOTAL TIME: **1 HOUR AND 30 MINUTES**

INGREDIENTS

3 LARGE EGGS

1 CUP SUGAR

¼ CUP HONEY

3 TABLESPOONS ALL-PURPOSE FLOUR

1 STICK UNSALTED BUTTER, MELTED AND SLIGHTLY COOLED

1¼ CUPS BUTTERMILK

1 TEASPOON PURE VANILLA EXTRACT

1 TABLESPOON FRESH LEMON JUICE

1 TEASPOON LEMON ZEST

¼ TEASPOON KOSHER SALT

1 PERFECT PIECRUST, BLIND BAKED (SEE PAGES 10–11)

DIRECTIONS

1. Preheat the oven to 350°F. Place all of the ingredients, except for the piecrust, in a mixing bowl and beat with a handheld mixer until thoroughly combined, about 3 to 4 minutes.

2. Pour the mixture into the piecrust, place the pie in the oven, and bake for about 45 minutes, until the filling is set and starting to brown. Remove from the oven and let cool slightly before serving.

CHAPTER 3

FRUIT

Chances are, your warmest pie-related memories are tied to one of the offerings in this chapter. Apple pie (see page 98) is so beloved that it has become inextricable from the very idea of America. The brevity of the season enabled blueberry pie to garner a day all its own (see page 123).

Those cornerstones, and the rest of the preparations in this section, prove that a pie is one of the best ways to capture the natural sweetness that Mother Nature has been so kind to bless the world with.

YIELD: **8 SERVINGS**

ACTIVE TIME: **35 MINUTES**

TOTAL TIME: **2 HOURS**

All-American Apple Pie

INGREDIENTS

8 CUPS PEELED AND SLICED APPLES

2 TABLESPOONS FRESH LEMON JUICE

½ CUP SUGAR

2 TEASPOONS CINNAMON

PINCH OF KOSHER SALT

¼ CUP ALL-PURPOSE FLOUR

2 PERFECT PIECRUSTS
(SEE PAGE 10)

1 EGG, BEATEN

DIRECTIONS

1. Place the apple slices, lemon juice, and sugar in a large saucepan and cook over medium heat until the apples start to soften, about 6 minutes.

2. Add the cinnamon and salt and cook for another minute. Strain the mixture through a fine sieve, reserve the liquid, and place the apples in a mixing bowl.

3. Return the reserved liquid to the saucepan and gradually add the flour while whisking to prevent lumps from forming. Cook until the liquid starts to thicken and stir it into the bowl containing the apples. Let the mixture cool completely. Preheat the oven to 350°F and grease a 9-inch pie plate.

4. Place one of the crusts in the prepared pie plate and then evenly distribute the apple mixture in the crust. Place the remaining crust on top, crimp the edge to seal, and cut four or five slits in the center. Brush the top crust with the beaten egg.

5. Place the pie in the oven and bake for about 45 minutes, until the top crust is golden brown and the filling is bubbling. Remove from the oven and let cool before serving.

APPLE OF YOUR EYE

While tradition recognizes the Granny Smith, with its tart taste and firm flesh, as the clear favorite, those who are fortunate to have access to the Northern Spy, which prefers cooler climates, swear that it is the best option when baking apple pies. Those who want straight sweetness in a pie trumpet the Honeycrisp, as it is not only sweet, but sturdy enough to not turn to mush in the oven.

YIELD: **8 SERVINGS**

ACTIVE TIME: **20 MINUTES**

TOTAL TIME: **1 HOUR AND 30 MINUTES**

Apple Pie with Quark

INGREDIENTS

1 PERFECT PIECRUST (SEE PAGE 10)

½ CUP GRANULATED SUGAR

1 STICK UNSALTED BUTTER, AT ROOM TEMPERATURE

3 LARGE EGGS, LIGHTLY BEATEN

2 CUPS QUARK CHEESE

1 TEASPOON PURE VANILLA EXTRACT

1 TEASPOON LEMON ZEST

1 TEASPOON FRESH LEMON JUICE

½ CUP ALL-PURPOSE FLOUR

1 TEASPOON BAKING POWDER

¼ TEASPOON KOSHER SALT

3 LARGE BRAEBURN APPLES, PEELED, CORED, AND HALVED

⅓ CUP SLIVERED ALMONDS

2 TABLESPOONS CONFECTIONERS' SUGAR

DIRECTIONS

1. Preheat the oven to 350°F, grease a 9-inch pie plate with nonstick cooking spray, and place the piecrust in it. Place the granulated sugar, butter, eggs, quark, vanilla, lemon zest, and lemon juice in a food processor and puree until smooth, scraping down the work bowl as needed.

2. Sift the flour, baking powder, and salt into a mixing bowl. Add the mixture to the food processor and pulse until incorporated. Evenly distribute the mixture in the crust and arrange the apples, cut-side down, in the mixture.

3. Place the pie in the oven and bake for about 40 minutes, until the filling is set and golden brown. Remove from the oven and let cool before serving. To serve, sprinkle the almonds and confectioners' sugar on top.

YIELD: **8 SERVINGS**

ACTIVE TIME: **15 MINUTES**

TOTAL TIME: **1 HOUR AND 30 MINUTES**

Apple & Pear Pie

INGREDIENTS

3 GRANNY SMITH APPLES, PEELED, CORED, AND SLICED

3 BARTLETT PEARS, PEELED, CORED, AND SLICED

½ TEASPOON CINNAMON

½ TEASPOON GROUND NUTMEG

½ CUP GRANULATED SUGAR

1 TEASPOON FRESH LEMON JUICE

1 TABLESPOON ALL-PURPOSE FLOUR

1 TABLESPOON UNSALTED BUTTER

1 TABLESPOON DARK BROWN SUGAR

2 PERFECT PIECRUSTS (SEE PAGE 10)

1 EGG WHITE

DIRECTIONS

1. Preheat the oven to 350°F. Place the apples, pears, cinnamon, nutmeg, granulated sugar, lemon juice, and flour in a mixing bowl and toss until the pieces of fruit are coated.

2. Place a 10-inch cast-iron skillet over medium heat and melt the butter in it. Add the brown sugar and cook, stirring constantly, until the sugar has dissolved. Remove the pan from heat and place one of the piecrusts over the sugar mixture. Fill the crust with the apple-and-pear mixture, place the other crust on top, and crimp the edge to seal. Brush the top crust with the egg white and cut four or five slits in the middle.

3. Place the skillet in the oven and bake for about 45 minutes, until the crust is golden brown and the filling is bubbling. Remove from the oven and let cool before serving.

Apple & Cranberry Pie

YIELD: **8 SERVINGS**

ACTIVE TIME: **20 MINUTES**

TOTAL TIME: **1 HOUR AND 15 MINUTES**

INGREDIENTS

2 PERFECT PIECRUSTS (SEE PAGE 10)

3 TABLESPOONS UNSALTED BUTTER

6 TART APPLES, PEELED, CORED, AND DICED

2 TABLESPOONS ALL-PURPOSE FLOUR

½ CUP GENTLY PACKED LIGHT BROWN SUGAR

1 TEASPOON CINNAMON

¼ TEASPOON GROUND NUTMEG

¼ TEASPOON KOSHER SALT

1 CUP WHOLE CRANBERRIES

½ CUP POMEGRANATE JUICE

1 CUP POMEGRANATE SEEDS

¼ CUP GRANULATED SUGAR

1 TABLESPOON FRESH LEMON JUICE

DIRECTIONS

1. Preheat the oven to 375°F. Grease a 9-inch pie plate with nonstick cooking spray and place one of the crusts in it.

2. Place the butter in a saucepan and melt over medium heat. Stir in the apples, flour, sugar, cinnamon, nutmeg, and salt and cook until the apples start to soften, about 6 minutes. Stir in the cranberries and cook, stirring occasionally, for another 2 minutes. Remove from heat and let the mixture cool.

3. While the apple mixture is cooling, place the pomegranate juice in a saucepan and cook over medium-high heat until it has reduced slightly, about 5 minutes. Stir in the pomegranate seeds, sugar, and lemon juice and cook until the sauce is viscous, about 5 minutes.

4. Pour the apple mixture into the crust in the pie plate. Drizzle the pomegranate sauce over the filling, place the other crust on top, crimp the edge to seal, and cut four or five slits in the center of the top crust. Place the pie in the oven and bake for about 45 minutes, until the top crust is golden brown. Remove and let cool briefly before serving.

YIELD: **8 SERVINGS**

ACTIVE TIME: **15 MINUTES**

TOTAL TIME: **1 HOUR AND 30 MINUTES**

Cherry & Apple Pie

INGREDIENTS

3 LARGE APPLES, PEELED, CORED, AND SLICED

1 TABLESPOON UNSALTED BUTTER

1 TABLESPOON FRESH LEMON JUICE

¼ TEASPOON GROUND GINGER

2 CUPS CHERRIES, PITTED AND CHOPPED OR PUREED

1 PERFECT PIECRUST, BLIND BAKED (SEE PAGE 10–11)

DIRECTIONS

1. Preheat the oven to 350°F.
2. Place the apples and butter in a skillet and cook over medium heat, while stirring, until the apples start to soften, about 10 minutes.
3. Transfer the apple pieces to a large bowl and add the lemon juice, ground ginger, and the cherries. Stir to combine and then evenly distribute the mixture in the piecrust.
4. Place the pie in the oven and bake for about 25 minutes, until the filling is heated through and set. Remove from the oven and let cool before serving.

YIELD: **8 SERVINGS**

ACTIVE TIME: **30 MINUTES**

TOTAL TIME: **1 HOUR AND 30 MINUTES**

Cherry Pie

INGREDIENTS

4 CUPS RAINIER CHERRIES, PITTED

2 CUPS SUGAR

2 TABLESPOONS FRESH LEMON JUICE

3 TABLESPOONS CORNSTARCH

1 TABLESPOON WATER

¼ TEASPOON PURE ALMOND EXTRACT

2 PERFECT PIECRUSTS (SEE PAGE 10)

1 EGG, BEATEN

DIRECTIONS

1. Place the cherries, sugar, and lemon juice in a saucepan and cook over medium heat, stirring occasionally, until the mixture is syrupy.

2. Combine the cornstarch and water in a small bowl and stir the slurry into the saucepan. Reduce the heat to low and cook, while stirring, until the mixture is thick. Remove from heat, stir in the almond extract, and let cool. Preheat the oven to 350°F.

3. When the cherry mixture has cooled, place one of the crusts in a greased 9-inch pie plate and pour the cherry mixture into the crust. Top with the other crust, make a few slits in the center, and brush the top crust with the beaten egg.

4. Place the pie in the oven and bake for about 45 minutes, until the top crust is golden brown. Remove from the oven and let the pie cool before serving.

YIELD: **8 SERVINGS**

ACTIVE TIME: **20 MINUTES**

TOTAL TIME: **1 HOUR AND 45 MINUTES**

Cherry Crumb Pie

INGREDIENTS

FOR THE PIE

4 CUPS RAINIER CHERRIES, PITTED

⅔ CUP SUGAR

2 TABLESPOONS CORNSTARCH

PINCH OF KOSHER SALT

1 TEASPOON PURE ALMOND EXTRACT

1 PERFECT PIECRUST, BLIND BAKED (SEE PAGES 10–11)

FOR THE TOPPING

1 CUP ALL-PURPOSE FLOUR

⅔ CUP CHOPPED ALMONDS, TOASTED

¾ CUP GENTLY PACKED LIGHT BROWN SUGAR

ZEST OF 1 SMALL LEMON

¼ TEASPOON KOSHER SALT

3 TABLESPOONS UNSALTED BUTTER, MELTED

DIRECTIONS

1. Preheat the oven to 350°F.
2. To begin preparations for the pie, place the cherries, sugar, cornstarch, salt, and almond extract in a mixing bowl and stir to combine. Pour the mixture into the blind-baked crust and use a rubber spatula to ensure that it is evenly distributed.
3. To prepare the topping, place the flour, almonds, sugar, lemon zest, and salt in the mixing bowl of a stand mixer fitted with the paddle attachment. Beat until combined and then, with the mixer running, slowly pour in the melted butter and beat until the mixture is moist and crumbly.
4. Sprinkle the topping over the cherry filling. Place the pie in the oven and bake for about 40 minutes, until the topping is golden brown and the filling is bubbling around the edges. Remove from the oven and let the pie cool before slicing and serving.

AT THE PINNACLE

While the cherry is loved in general, the support for the Rainier cherry borders on reverence. After drawing people in with the sunset hues of its skin, the Rainier pays off that intrigue with amazingly creamy flesh and unparalleled sweetness.

That next-level existence is hard won. The Rainier is incredibly delicate, requiring considerable patience and a pioneering spirit of anyone who chooses to cultivate it. A gust of wind or a heavy rainfall can damage the cherry's fragile skin, and if the temperature hits 90°F , the cherry loses a day of life. If one can weather those swings, a crop of perfect cherries will result–for two months. The brevity of the season sends cherry lovers into a tizzy, resulting in high prices that can make the delicate fruit seem well worth the gamble it requires.

Named for the truly awesome mountain that looms large on the Seattle skyline, the Rainier is a cross between two varieties of sweet red cherries—a Bing and a Van—that Harold Fogle, a professor at Washington State University, produced in 1952. Fogle's matchmaking was spot on in this instance, as he produced a cherry that occasionally goes for $1 a piece in Japan.

YIELD: **8 SERVINGS**

ACTIVE TIME: **30 MINUTES**

TOTAL TIME: **2 HOURS**

Sour Cherry Pie

INGREDIENTS

1 PERFECT PIECRUST (SEE PAGE 10)

3¾ CUPS MONTMORENCY CHERRIES, PITTED

2¾ CUPS GRANULATED SUGAR

2½ TABLESPOONS WATER

¼ CUP CORNSTARCH

½ CUP ALL-PURPOSE FLOUR

½ CUP FIRMLY PACKED DARK BROWN SUGAR

⅔ CUP OATS

6 TABLESPOONS UNSALTED BUTTER, CHILLED AND CUT INTO SMALL PIECES

DIRECTIONS

1. Grease a 9-inch pie plate with nonstick cooking spray and place the crust in it.
2. Place cherries and the granulated sugar in a saucepan and cook over medium heat, stirring constantly, until the sugar has dissolved, about 5 minutes.
3. Place the water and cornstarch in a bowl and stir to combine. Stir the slurry into the saucepan and cook until the mixture becomes viscous. Remove the pan from heat and let the mixture cool completely. Preheat the oven to 350°F.
4. Add the sour cherry filling to the crust and set the pie aside.
5. Place the flour, brown sugar, oats, and butter in a mixing bowl and work the mixture until it is combined and crumbly. Spread the mixture over the filling, place the pie in the oven, and bake for about 45 minutes, until the crust and topping are golden brown and the filling is bubbling. Remove from the oven and let cool before serving.

YIELD: **8 SERVINGS**

ACTIVE TIME: **15 MINUTES**

TOTAL TIME: **1 HOUR AND 30 MINUTES**

Peach Pie

INGREDIENTS

2 PERFECT PIECRUSTS (SEE PAGE 10)

4 CUPS PEELED, PITTED, AND SLICED PEACHES

1 TEASPOON FRESH LEMON JUICE

¾ CUP SUGAR, PLUS 2 TABLESPOONS

¼ CUP ALL-PURPOSE FLOUR

1 EGG WHITE, LIGHTLY BEATEN

DIRECTIONS

1. Preheat the oven to 350°F. Grease a 9-inch pie plate with nonstick cooking spray and place one of the piecrusts in it.
2. Place the peaches, lemon juice, the ¾ cup of sugar, and the flour in a mixing bowl and stir until the peach slices are evenly coated.
3. Evenly distribute the mixture in the piecrust. Place the other piecrust over the mixture and crimp the edges to seal.
4. Brush the top crust with the egg white and sprinkle the remaining sugar over it. Cut four or five slits in the center of the crust, place the pie in the oven, and bake for about 45 minutes, until the top crust is golden brown and the filling is bubbling. Remove from the oven and let cool before serving.

NOTE: A dollop of bourbon-spiked whipped cream is outstanding on top of this pie. Just add 1 tablespoon of bourbon to the ingredients for the Whipped Cream on page 38 and proceed as directed.

Plum Pie with Hazelnut Crumble

YIELD: **8 SERVINGS**

ACTIVE TIME: **20 MINUTES**

TOTAL TIME: **1 HOUR AND 30 MINUTES**

INGREDIENTS

FOR THE PIE

1 PERFECT PIECRUST (SEE PAGE 10)

2 TABLESPOONS UNSALTED BUTTER

10 RIPE PLUMS, PITTED AND HALVED

½ CUP SUGAR

¼ CUP WATER

2 TABLESPOONS CORNSTARCH

1 TABLESPOON FRESH LEMON JUICE

FOR THE CRUMBLE

¼ CUP LIGHT BROWN SUGAR

¼ CUP SUGAR

½ CUP ALL-PURPOSE FLOUR

⅓ CUP ALMOND MEAL

3 TABLESPOONS UNSALTED BUTTER

¼ TEASPOON GROUND CINNAMON

¼ TEASPOON KOSHER SALT

⅓ CUP BLANCHED HAZELNUTS, CHOPPED

DIRECTIONS

1. Preheat the oven to 350°F. To begin preparations for the pie, grease a 9-inch pie plate with nonstick cooking spray and place the piecrust in it.

2. Place the butter in a saucepan and melt over medium heat. Add the plums, sugar, and water and cook, stirring occasionally, until the plums start to break down, 7 to 10 minutes. Remove from heat and stir in the cornstarch and lemon juice. Evenly distribute the mixture in the piecrust, making sure the plums are cut-side up.

3. To prepare the crumble,place all of the ingredients, except for the hazelnuts, in a food processor and pulse until the mixture is a coarse meal. Spread the mixture over the pie and sprinkle the hazelnuts on top.

4. Place the pie in the oven and bake for about 45 minutes, until the crumble is golden brown. Remove from the oven and let cool before serving.

YIELD: **8 SERVINGS**

ACTIVE TIME: **20 MINUTES**

TOTAL TIME: **1 HOUR AND 30 MINUTES**

Strawberry Rhubarb Pie

INGREDIENTS

2 PERFECT PIECRUSTS (SEE PAGE 10)

4 CUPS HULLED AND HALVED STRAWBERRIES

4 CUPS CHOPPED RHUBARB

1 CUP SUGAR

¼ CUP CORNSTARCH

ZEST OF ½ ORANGE

PINCH OF KOSHER SALT

2 TABLESPOONS UNSALTED BUTTER, CUT INTO SMALL PIECES

1 EGG, BEATEN

DIRECTIONS

1. Preheat the oven to 400°F. Grease a 9-inch pie plate with nonstick cooking spray and place one of the crusts in it.
2. Place the strawberries, rhubarb, sugar, cornstarch, orange zest, and salt in a large mixing bowl and stir to combine. Evenly distribute the mixture in the crust and dot the mixture with the butter.
3. Cut the other crust into 1-inch-wide strips. Lay some of the strips over the pie and trim the strips so that they fit. To make a lattice crust, lift every other strip and fold them back so you can place another strip across those strips that remain flat. Lay the folded strips back down over the cross-strip. Fold back the strips that you laid the cross-strip on top of, and repeat until the lattice covers the surface of the pie. Brush the lattice crust, taking care not to get any egg on the filling.
4. Place the pie on a baking sheet, place it in the oven, and bake for 20 minutes. Reduce the temperature to 350°F and bake for about 40 minutes, until the filling is bubbling and the crust is golden brown. Remove and let cool before serving.

YIELD: **8 SERVINGS**

ACTIVE TIME: **40 MINUTES**

TOTAL TIME: **4 HOURS**

Strawberry Pie

INGREDIENTS

¾ CUP SUGAR

3 TABLESPOONS CORNSTARCH

½ CUP WATER

6 CUPS FRESH STRAWBERRIES, HULLED AND HALVED

1 PERFECT PIECRUST, BLIND BAKED (SEE PAGES 10–11)

½ CUP UNSWEETENED STRAWBERRY PRESERVES

VANILLA ICE CREAM, FOR SERVING

DIRECTIONS

1. Place the sugar, cornstarch, and water in a saucepan and cook over medium heat, stirring constantly. When the sugar and cornstarch have dissolved, stir in 1 cup of the strawberries and cook, while stirring, until the mixture begins to thicken and come to a boil. Continue to cook and stir the mixture for 5 minutes. Remove the saucepan from heat and let cool for 20 minutes.
2. Place the remaining strawberry pieces in even layers in the blind-baked crust. When the mixture in the saucepan has cooled, pour it over the strawberries.
3. Place the strawberry preserves in a microwave-safe bowl. Microwave on medium until just melted, about 20 seconds. Stir and drizzle over the pie.
4. Cover the pie with plastic wrap and place in the refrigerator for at least 3 hours before serving. To serve, place a scoop of vanilla ice cream on top of each slice.

YIELD: **8 SERVINGS**

ACTIVE TIME: **30 MINUTES**

TOTAL TIME: **1 HOUR AND 30 MINUTES**

Blueberry Pie

INGREDIENTS

6 CUPS FRESH OR FROZEN BLUEBERRIES

1 TABLESPOON FRESH LEMON JUICE

1 TEASPOON LEMON ZEST

¾ CUP SUGAR, PLUS 2 TABLESPOONS

2 PERFECT PIECRUSTS (SEE PAGE 10)

1 EGG WHITE, LIGHTLY BEATEN

DIRECTIONS

1. Preheat the oven to 350°F.

2. Place the blueberries, lemon juice, lemon zest, and the ¾ cup of sugar in a large mixing bowl and stir to combine.

3. Place one of the crusts in a greased 9-inch pie plate and fill it with the blueberry mixture. Place the other crust over the mixture and crimp the edge to seal.

4. Brush the top crust with the egg white and then sprinkle the remaining sugar over it. Cut four or five slits in the middle, place the pie in the oven, and bake for about 45 minutes, until the top crust is golden brown and the filling is bubbling. Remove from the oven and let cool before serving.

A DAY TO REMEMBER

For many people, pie is associated with a specific holiday or time of year: apple pie in October, pumpkin and pecan pies on Thanksgiving, and strawberry rhubarb pie as the summer gets underway.

But a pie getting official recognition and being honored with a day of its own means that it resides on an entirely different level. The blueberry pie has been regarded as such, using its considerable charm to transcend mere tradition and claim April 28 as National Blueberry Pie Day. Interestingly, this is far too early for those who live in Maine—where blueberry pie is the official state dessert—to enjoy a slice made with fresh berries, as blueberry season in the New England state typically runs from July to September.

YIELD: **8 SERVINGS**

ACTIVE TIME: **30 MINUTES**

TOTAL TIME: **1 HOUR AND 45 MINUTES**

Mixed Berry Pie

INGREDIENTS

2 PERFECT PIECRUSTS (SEE PAGE 10)

1½ CUPS FRESH BLUEBERRIES

1 CUP FRESH BLACKBERRIES

1 CUP FRESH RASPBERRIES

1½ CUPS FRESH STRAWBERRIES, HULLED AND HALVED

1 TABLESPOON FRESH LEMON JUICE

½ CUP GENTLY PACKED LIGHT BROWN SUGAR

2 TABLESPOONS CORNSTARCH

½ CUP UNSWEETENED RASPBERRY PRESERVES

1 EGG, BEATEN

DIRECTIONS

1. Preheat the oven to 375°F, grease a 9-inch pie plate with nonstick cooking spray, and place one of the crusts in it.

2. Place all of the berries and the lemon juice, brown sugar, and cornstarch in a large bowl and toss to combine. Transfer the fruit to a large saucepan and cook over medium heat until the berries start to break down, 7 to 10 minutes. Stir in the preserves, remove the pan from heat, and set the mixture aside.

3. Pour the berry mixture into the crust and cut the other crust into 1-inch-wide strips. Lay some of the strips over the pie and trim any excess. To make a lattice crust, lift every other strip and fold back so you can place another strip across those strips that remain flat. Lay the folded strips back down over the cross-strip. Fold back the strips that you laid the cross-strip on top of, and repeat until the lattice covers the surface of the pie. Brush the strips with the beaten egg, taking care not to get any egg on the filling.

4. Place the pie in the oven and bake for 45 minutes, until the crust is golden brown and the filling is bubbling. Remove from the oven and let cool before serving.

YIELD: **8 SERVINGS**

ACTIVE TIME: **30 MINUTES**

TOTAL TIME: **2 HOURS AND 45 MINUTES**

Linzer Pie

INGREDIENTS

1 CUP SUGAR

1½ STICKS UNSALTED BUTTER, AT ROOM TEMPERATURE

1 TEASPOON LEMON ZEST

3 EGGS

1¼ CUPS ALL-PURPOSE FLOUR, PLUS MORE AS NEEDED

1 CUP ALMOND MEAL, LIGHTLY TOASTED

½ TEASPOON CINNAMON

¼ TEASPOON GROUND CLOVES

1 TABLESPOON UNSWEETENED COCOA POWDER

¼ TEASPOON KOSHER SALT

1½ CUPS RASPBERRY JAM

DIRECTIONS

1. Place the sugar, butter, and lemon zest in a mixing bowl and beat with a handheld mixer until the mixture is pale and fluffy. Incorporate two of the eggs, adding one at a time and scraping down the mixing bowl as needed.

2. Place the flour, almond meal, cinnamon, ground cloves, cocoa powder, and salt in a separate bowl and whisk to combine. Gradually add this mixture to the wet mixture and stir until the dough just holds together. Divide the dough in half, envelop each piece in plastic wrap, and refrigerate for 1 hour.

3. Preheat the oven to 350°F and grease a 9-inch pie plate with nonstick cooking spray. Place the pieces of dough on a flour-dusted work surface and roll them out to fit the pie plate. Place one piece of dough in the pie plate and then cut the other piece of dough into ¾-inch-wide strips.

4. Fill the crust in the pie plate with the raspberry jam. Lay some of the strips over the pie and trim any excess. To make a lattice crust, lift every other strip and fold back so you can place another strip across those strips that remain flat. Lay the folded strips back down over the cross-strip. Fold back the strips that you laid the cross-strip on top of, and repeat until the lattice covers the surface of the pie. Beat the remaining egg until scrambled and brush the strips with it, taking care not to get any egg on the filling.

5. Place the pie in the oven and bake for about 45 minutes, until the crust is golden brown. Remove from the oven and let cool before serving.

YIELD: **8 SERVINGS**

ACTIVE TIME: **15 MINUTES**

TOTAL TIME: **1 HOUR AND 30 MINUTES**

Raspberry Pie

INGREDIENTS

2 PERFECT PIECRUSTS (SEE PAGE 10)

⅔ CUP ALL-PURPOSE FLOUR

7 CUPS FRESH RASPBERRIES

2 CUPS SUGAR, PLUS MORE TO TASTE

2 TABLESPOONS FRESH LEMON JUICE

PINCH OF KOSHER SALT

1 EGG, BEATEN

DIRECTIONS

1. Preheat the oven to 350°F. Grease a 9-inch pie plate and place one of the crusts in it.
2. Place the flour, raspberries, sugar, lemon juice, and salt in a mixing bowl and stir until well combined. Evenly distribute this mixture in the crust in the pie plate.
3. Place the top crust over the filling, trim any excess, and crimp the edge to seal. Brush the top crust with the egg, make four or five slits in it, and sprinkle additional sugar on top.
4. Place the pie in the oven and bake until the crust is golden brown, about 45 minutes. Remove from the oven and let cool before serving.

YIELD: **8 SERVINGS**

ACTIVE TIME: **15 MINUTES**

TOTAL TIME: **1 HOUR AND 30 MINUTES**

Black Raspberry Pie

INGREDIENTS

2 PERFECT PIECRUSTS (SEE PAGE 10)

7 CUPS FRESH BLACK RASPBERRIES

1½ CUPS SUGAR, PLUS MORE TO TASTE

1 TABLESPOON FRESH LEMON JUICE

PINCH OF KOSHER SALT

1 EGG, BEATEN

DIRECTIONS

1. Preheat the oven to 350°F. Grease a 9-inch pie plate and place one of the crusts in it.
2. Place the black raspberries, sugar, lemon juice, and salt in a mixing bowl and stir until well combined. Evenly distribute this mixture in the crust in the pie plate.
3. Place the top crust over the filling, trim any excess, and crimp the edge to seal. Brush the top crust with the egg, make four or five slits in it, and sprinkle additional sugar on top.
4. Place the pie in the oven and bake until the crust is golden brown, about 45 minutes. Remove from the oven and let cool before serving.

SHADES OF BLACK

Rarely seen outside of the ice cream stand, most folks assume that the black raspberry is just another name for the blackberries they regularly encounter at the farmers market or grocery store.

But despite the similarities in appearance, there are a few crucial differences. The black raspberry is less tart than the blackberry and its red counterpart. The black raspberry is fruitier and also not as sweet as the blackberry, which has high levels of sugar. This diminished sweetness and tartness lend the flavor of the black raspberry a floral quality that shines in a rich, custardy ice cream.

That said, taste is not the only way to recognize the difference between the two: the black raspberry will have small hairs and will be hollow inside, since it comes directly off the bush, as opposed to the blackberry, which must be pulled from a stem.

YIELD: **8 SERVINGS**

ACTIVE TIME: **30 MINUTES**

TOTAL TIME: **1 HOUR AND 45 MINUTES**

Blackberry Pie

INGREDIENTS

2 CUPS SLIVERED ALMONDS

⅓ CUP ALL-PURPOSE FLOUR

½ CUP GRANULATED SUGAR

⅔ CUP UNSWEETENED COCOA POWDER

¾ CUP UNSALTED BUTTER, SOFTENED

2 CUPS BLACKBERRIES

1 CUP CONFECTIONERS' SUGAR

1 TABLESPOON FRESH LEMON JUICE

4 LARGE EGG WHITES, AT ROOM TEMPERATURE

1 COCOA CRUST (SEE PAGE 17)

DIRECTIONS

1. Preheat the oven to 350°F. Place the almonds, flour, ¼ cup of the granulated sugar, and the cocoa powder in a food processor and pulse until the almonds are very finely ground. Add the butter and pulse until incorporated. Place the mixture in a mixing bowl and set aside.

2. Wipe out the food processor, add 1½ cups of the blackberries, ½ cup of the confectioners' sugar, and the lemon juice and puree until smooth. Strain through a fine sieve to remove as many seeds from the puree as possible. Set the puree aside.

3. Place the egg whites in a mixing bowl and beat until foamy. Gradually add the remaining granulated sugar and beat until the mixture holds soft peaks. Whisk about one-third of the meringue into the almond mixture. Fold in the remaining meringue and the blackberry puree. Evenly distribute the mixture in the crust.

4. Place the pie in the oven and bake for about 45 minutes, until the filling is set and dry to the touch. Remove from the oven and let cool. To serve, sprinkle the remaining confectioners' sugar over the pie and arrange the remaining blackberries on top.

YIELD: **8 SERVINGS**

ACTIVE TIME: **20 MINUTES**

TOTAL TIME: **2 HOURS**

Grape Pie

INGREDIENTS

2 PERFECT PIECRUSTS (SEE PAGE 10)

4 CUPS SEEDLESS RED GRAPES, HALVED

⅔ CUP SUGAR

3 TABLESPOONS CORNSTARCH

2 TABLESPOONS FRESH LEMON JUICE

2 TABLESPOONS UNSALTED BUTTER

2 TABLESPOONS MILK

DIRECTIONS

1. Preheat the oven to 350°F. Grease a 9-inch pie plate with nonstick cooking spray and place one of the crusts in it. Place the grapes and sugar in a saucepan and let the mixture stand for 15 minutes.

2. Place the cornstarch and lemon juice in a small bowl and whisk to combine. Pour the slurry into the saucepan, add the butter, and stir to combine. Cook over medium heat, stirring frequently, until the grapes start to collapse, about 4 minutes. Remove from heat and let the mixture cool slightly.

3. Evenly distribute the grape mixture in the crust in the pie plate. Place the remaining crust on top, crimp the edge to seal, and make a hole in the center of the pie. Brush the top crust with the milk.

4. Place the pie in the oven and bake for about 45 minutes, until the crust is golden brown and the filling is bubbling. Remove from the oven and let cool before serving.

YIELD: **8 SERVINGS**

ACTIVE TIME: **20 MINUTES**

TOTAL TIME: **2 HOURS**

Raisin Pie

INGREDIENTS

2 PERFECT PIECRUSTS (SEE PAGE 10)

2 CUPS RAISINS

2 CUPS WATER

½ CUP GENTLY PACKED DARK BROWN SUGAR

2 TABLESPOONS CORNSTARCH

1½ TEASPOONS GROUND CINNAMON

¼ TEASPOON KOSHER SALT

1 TABLESPOON PURE VANILLA EXTRACT

1 TABLESPOON WHITE VINEGAR

1 TABLESPOON UNSALTED BUTTER

⅔ CUP BLANCHED HAZELNUTS

1 LARGE EGG, BEATEN

1 TABLESPOON MILK

1 TABLESPOON GRANULATED SUGAR

DIRECTIONS

1. Preheat the oven to 350°F. Grease a 9-inch pie plate with nonstick cooking spray and place one of the piecrusts in it. Place the raisins and water in a saucepan and bring to a boil over medium heat. Cook for 5 minutes, stirring occasionally. Stir in the brown sugar, cornstarch, cinnamon, salt, and vanilla, reduce heat to medium-low, and cook until the mixture is syrupy. Remove from heat and stir in the vinegar, butter, and hazelnuts. Let the mixture cool for 5 to 10 minutes.

2. Evenly distribute the raisin mixture in the piecrust. Place the remaining piecrust on top, crimp the edge to seal, and cut four or five slits in the center. Place the egg and milk in a small bowl, beat until combined, and then brush the top crust with the egg wash. Sprinkle the granulated sugar over the crust.

3. Place the pie in the oven and bake for about 45 minutes, until the crust is golden brown. Remove from the oven and let cool before serving.

Shaker Lemon Pie

YIELD: **8 SERVINGS**

ACTIVE TIME: **15 MINUTES**

TOTAL TIME: **4 HOURS AND 30 MINUTES**

INGREDIENTS

2 LEMONS, WASHED AND DRIED

2 CUPS SUGAR, PLUS 1 TABLESPOON

2 PERFECT PIECRUSTS (SEE PAGE 10)

4 LARGE EGGS, THOROUGHLY BEATEN

2 TABLESPOONS ALL-PURPOSE FLOUR

¼ TEASPOON KOSHER SALT

2 TABLESPOONS MILK

DIRECTIONS

1. Trim the ends from the lemons. Cut each lemon, crosswise, into very thin slices—a mandoline is ideal for this. Chop the lemons and place any juice in a mixing bowl. Add the sugar and toss to combine. Cover and let the mixture stand at room temperature for at least 3 hours, stirring occasionally.

2. Preheat the oven to 425°F, grease a 9-inch pie plate with nonstick cooking spray, and place one of the crusts in it. Stir the eggs, flour, and salt into the lemon mixture. Spoon the filling into the crust, place the other crust on top, and crimp the edge to seal. Brush the top crust with the milk and cut four or five slits in it.

3. Place the pie in the oven and bake for 15 minutes. Reduce the temperature to 350°F and bake for another 30 minutes, until the top crust is golden brown. Remove from the oven and let cool before serving.

CHAPTER 4

NUTTY

Anyone who has ever sank into the unparalleled richness of a pecan pie understands that those pies based around the versatile nut are so delicious and decadent that they almost feel criminal. In addition to several twists on this Southern staple, there's also a mind-blowing Elvis-inspired pie (see page 152), and one that takes its cue from another famed treat—the peanut butter cup (see page 151).

That nutty moniker also applies to a few pies so innovative that they are otherwise uncategorizable—a motley crew that includes the Crack Pie made famous by David Chang and the team at New York's Momofuku Milk Bar (see page 158).

YIELD: **8 SERVINGS**

ACTIVE TIME: **20 MINUTES**

TOTAL TIME: **1 HOUR AND 30 MINUTES**

Pecan Pie

INGREDIENTS

1 PERFECT PIECRUST (SEE PAGE 10)

1 CUP LIGHT CORN SYRUP

1 CUP GENTLY PACKED DARK BROWN SUGAR

3 EGGS, LIGHTLY BEATEN

⅓ CUP UNSALTED BUTTER, MELTED

½ TEASPOON KOSHER SALT

1 CUP PECAN HALVES

DIRECTIONS

1. Preheat the oven to 350°F, grease a 9-inch pie plate with nonstick cooking spray, and place the piecrust in it. Chill in the refrigerator for 15 minutes.

2. Place the remaining ingredients in a large mixing bowl and stir until combined. Evenly distribute the mixture in the crust.

3. Place the pie in the oven and bake for about 45 minutes, until the crust is golden brown and the filling is set. Remove from the oven and let cool before serving.

Salted Caramel & Pecan Pie

YIELD: **8 SERVINGS**

ACTIVE TIME: **25 MINUTES**

TOTAL TIME: **1 HOUR AND 30 MINUTES**

INGREDIENTS

1 PERFECT PIECRUST (SEE PAGE 10)

½ CUP CHOPPED PECANS

1½ CUPS MIXED SALTED NUTS

1¾ CUPS SUGAR

⅓ CUP DARK CORN SYRUP

¼ CUP WATER

¾ CUP HEAVY CREAM

2 TABLESPOONS DARK RUM

1 TEASPOON KOSHER SALT

3 LARGE EGGS, BEATEN

DIRECTIONS

1. Preheat the oven to 350°F. Grease a 9-inch pie plate with nonstick cooking spray and place the piecrust in it. Place the pecans and the mixed nuts in a bowl and stir to combine. Set the mixture aside.

2. Place the sugar, corn syrup, and water in a saucepan and cook over medium heat, stirring constantly, until the sugar has dissolved. Raise the heat to medium-high and continue to stir until the mixture comes to a boil and begins to turn dark brown, about 10 minutes. Remove the saucepan from heat and stir in the cream, being careful as the mixture will spatter.

3. Place the saucepan over medium-low heat, add the rum and salt, and cook, while stirring, until the mixture is smooth. Ladle into a large bowl and let cool.

4. When the mixture is cool, whisk in the eggs and pour the mixture into the piecrust. Sprinkle the nut mixture over the top, place in the oven, and bake for about 45 minutes, until the filling is set. Remove from the oven and let cool before serving.

Chocolate & Bourbon Pecan Pie

YIELD: **8 SERVINGS**

ACTIVE TIME: **25 MINUTES**

TOTAL TIME: **1 HOUR AND 30 MINUTES**

INGREDIENTS

1½ CUPS CHOPPED PECANS, TOASTED

1 CUP SEMISWEET CHOCOLATE CHIPS

1 COCOA CRUST (SEE PAGE 17)

1 CUP DARK CORN SYRUP

⅓ CUP GRANULATED SUGAR

½ CUP FIRMLY PACKED LIGHT BROWN SUGAR

¼ CUP BOURBON

4 LARGE EGGS, BEATEN

DIRECTIONS

1. Preheat the oven to 325°F. Evenly distribute the pecans and chocolate chips in the piecrust.
2. Place the corn syrup, granulated sugar, light brown sugar, and bourbon in a saucepan and cook, stirring constantly, over medium heat until the mixture comes to a boil. Remove the saucepan from heat. Working in four increments, whisk the mixture into the eggs. When all of the mixture has been incorporated, pour the tempered eggs into the piecrust.
3. Place the pie in the oven and bake for about 1 hour, until the filling is set. Remove from the oven and let cool before serving.

YIELD: **8 SERVINGS**

ACTIVE TIME: **20 MINUTES**

TOTAL TIME: **1 HOUR AND 30 MINUTES**

Walnut Pie

INGREDIENTS

1 PERFECT PIECRUST (SEE PAGE 10)

2½ CUPS MINCED WALNUTS

¼ CUP GENTLY PACKED DARK BROWN SUGAR

2 TABLESPOONS GRANULATED SUGAR

1½ TEASPOONS CINNAMON

1 STICK UNSALTED BUTTER, MELTED

¾ CUP HONEY

1 TABLESPOON FRESH LEMON JUICE

DIRECTIONS

1. Preheat the oven to 325°F. Grease a 9-inch pie plate with nonstick cooking spray and place the piecrust in it.
2. Place the walnuts, brown sugar, granulated sugar, and cinnamon in a mixing bowl and stir to combine.
3. Drizzle half of the melted butter over the crust and then spread the walnut mixture evenly on top. Pour the remaining butter over the walnut mixture, place the pie in the oven, and bake for about 50 minutes, until the crust is golden brown. Remove from the oven and let the pie cool slightly.
4. Place the honey and lemon juice in a small saucepan and warm over medium heat, stirring constantly, until the mixture acquires a watery consistency. Drizzle the mixture over the pie and let the pie cool completely before serving.

YIELD: **8 SERVINGS**

ACTIVE TIME: **15 MINUTES**

TOTAL TIME: **2 HOURS AND 15 MINUTES**

Peanut Butter Pie

INGREDIENTS

3 EGGS

1 CUP DARK CORN SYRUP

½ CUP SUGAR

1½ CUPS SMOOTH ALL-NATURAL PEANUT BUTTER

½ TEASPOON PURE VANILLA EXTRACT

1 GRAHAM CRACKER CRUST (SEE PAGE 25)

1 CUP SEMISWEET CHOCOLATE CHIPS

DIRECTIONS

1. Preheat the oven to 350°F. Place the eggs in a large bowl and whisk until scrambled. Add the corn syrup and sugar and whisk until the sugar has dissolved. Add the peanut butter and vanilla and whisk until the mixture is smooth and just combined.

2. Evenly distribute the mixture in the crust. Place the pie in the oven and bake for about 1 hour, until the filling is set. Remove from the oven and let cool.

3. Place the chocolate chips in a microwave-safe bowl and microwave on medium until melted, removing to stir every 15 seconds. Spread the melted chocolate evenly over the pie and chill in the refrigerator until the chocolate has hardened, about 45 minutes.

YIELD: **8 SERVINGS**

ACTIVE TIME: **20 MINUTES**

TOTAL TIME: **1 HOUR**

Graceland Pie

INGREDIENTS

¾ CUP SUGAR

⅓ CUP ALL-PURPOSE FLOUR

¼ TEASPOON KOSHER SALT

2 CUPS WHOLE MILK

3 EGG YOLKS, BEATEN

2 TABLESPOONS UNSALTED BUTTER

1¼ TEASPOONS PURE VANILLA EXTRACT

4 BANANAS, SLICED

¼ CUP SMOOTH PEANUT BUTTER

1 GRAHAM CRACKER CRUST (SEE PAGE 25, MADE WITH CHOCOLATE GRAHAM CRACKERS)

1½ CUPS WHIPPED CREAM (SEE PAGE 38)

DEHYDRATED BANANA CHIPS, FOR GARNISH

¼ CUP CRISPY, CHOPPED BACON, FOR GARNISH (OPTIONAL)

DIRECTIONS

1. Place the sugar, flour, and salt in a saucepan and whisk to combine. Whisk the milk into the mixture and bring to a simmer over medium heat, stirring constantly, for 2 minutes. Remove from heat.

2. While whisking constantly, stir a small amount of the warmed mixture into the beaten egg yolks. Add the tempered egg yolks to the saucepan, place the pan back over medium heat, and cook until the mixture thickens and starts bubbling, while whisking constantly. Remove from heat and stir in the butter and vanilla. Add half of the sliced bananas, stir to coat, and let the mixture cool.

3. While the mixture is cooling, place the peanut butter in a saucepan and warm over medium heat until it starts to liquefy.

4. Place the remaining bananas in the piecrust and then pour the cooled banana cream on top. Cover with the Whipped Cream, drizzle the warmed peanut butter on top, and arrange the dehydrated banana chips and bacon pieces (if using) on top.

FIT FOR A KING

The size of Elvis Presley's legend means that we are far better acquainted with his daily routine and peccadillos than one might expect. While Elvis had a number of outsized appetites—including for something he tabbed the "Fool's Gold Loaf," a loaf of Italian bread filled with a pound of bacon, peanut butter, and jelly—none is better known than his love of fried peanut butter, banana, and bacon sandwiches. Elvis scribes are divided on whether his mother, or his longtime cook, Pauline Nicholson, is responsible for cultivating this hunger in Elvis, and whether the bananas should be caramelized in a frying pan in the canonical version. But, as anyone brave enough to try the bizarre trio knows, "The King" was preternaturally attuned to recognize a hit.

YIELD: **8 SERVINGS**

ACTIVE TIME: **30 MINUTES**

TOTAL TIME: **2 HOURS AND 30 MINUTES**

Nutty Butterscotch Pie

INGREDIENTS

1 STICK UNSALTED BUTTER

1¼ CUPS GENTLY PACKED LIGHT BROWN SUGAR

1½ CUPS WATER

¼ CUP CORNSTARCH

3 TABLESPOONS ALL-PURPOSE FLOUR

½ TEASPOON KOSHER SALT

1½ CUPS HEAVY CREAM

½ CUP WHOLE MILK

4 EGG YOLKS, BEATEN

1 TEASPOON PURE VANILLA EXTRACT

1 SWEET CRUST (SEE PAGE 13)

1 CUP PECANS, TOASTED

BUTTERSCOTCH CANDIES, CRUSHED, FOR GARNISH

DIRECTIONS

1. Place the butter in a saucepan and melt over medium heat. Stir in the brown sugar and water and cook, stirring frequently, until the mixture comes to a boil. Remove from heat and set aside.

2. Place the cornstarch, flour, and salt in a mixing bowl and stir to combine. Add ½ cup of the cream and stir to combine. Stir in the remaining cup of cream and the milk and then whisk the mixture into the mixture in the saucepan. Place the saucepan over medium heat and cook, stirring constantly, until the mixture thickens, about 3 minutes.

3. Whisk a ladleful of the mixture in the saucepan into the egg yolks. Whisk in another ladleful of the mixture and then stir the tempered egg yolks into the saucepan. Cook for another minute, while whisking constantly, remove from heat, and stir in the vanilla.

4. Evenly distribute the mixture in the crust, cover the pie with plastic wrap, and refrigerate for 2 hours. Arrange the toasted pecans and butterscotch pieces on top when ready to serve.

YIELD: **8 TO 10 SERVINGS**

ACTIVE TIME: **1 HOUR**

TOTAL TIME: **6 HOURS AND 30 MINUTES**

Boston Cream Pie

INGREDIENTS

FOR THE FILLING

½ CUP SUGAR

PINCH OF KOSHER SALT

6 LARGE EGG YOLKS

¼ CUP ALL-PURPOSE FLOUR

2 CUPS HALF-AND-HALF

4 TABLESPOONS UNSALTED BUTTER, CHILLED AND DIVIDED INTO TABLESPOONS

SEEDS OF 1 VANILLA BEAN

FOR THE FROSTING

½ CUP HEAVY CREAM

2 TABLESPOONS LIGHT CORN SYRUP

1 CUP BITTERSWEET CHOCOLATE CHIPS

Continued...

DIRECTIONS

1. To begin preparations for the filling, place the sugar, salt, and egg yolks in a mixing bowl and whisk until smooth. Add the flour and whisk to incorporate.
2. Place the half-and-half in a saucepan and bring to a simmer over medium heat. Remove the pan from heat and slowly pour ½ cup into the flour-and-egg yolk mixture while whisking constantly. Whisk the tempered mixture into the half-and-half that remains in the saucepan. Place the saucepan over medium heat and cook, whisking constantly, until the mixture thickens, about 1 minute. Reduce heat to medium-low and simmer, while whisking constantly, for 8 minutes.
3. Raise the heat to medium and cook, while whisking vigorously, until the mixture starts to bubble, 1 to 2 minutes. Remove saucepan from heat, add the butter and vanilla seeds, and whisk until the butter is melted and incorporated. Strain through a fine sieve and let cool. When cool, press plastic wrap directly onto the surface of the custard and place in the refrigerator for 2 hours.
4. To prepare the frosting, place the cream and corn syrup in a small saucepan and bring to a simmer over medium heat. When the mixture is simmering, remove from heat and add the chocolate. Gently whisk until smooth and set aside.
5. To begin preparations for the cakes, preheat the oven to 325°F. Grease two round 9-inch cake pans with nonstick cooking spray and line them with parchment paper. Place the flour, baking powder, and salt in mixing bowl and whisk to combine. Place the milk and butter in a small saucepan and warm over low heat until the butter has melted. Remove from heat, stir in the vanilla, and cover.

Continued...

FOR THE CAKES

1½ CUPS ALL-PURPOSE FLOUR

1½ TEASPOONS BAKING POWDER

¾ TEASPOON KOSHER SALT

¾ CUP WHOLE MILK

6 TABLESPOONS UNSALTED BUTTER

1½ TEASPOONS PURE VANILLA EXTRACT

3 LARGE EGGS

1½ CUPS SUGAR

6. Place the eggs and sugar in the bowl of a stand mixer and beat on high until the mixture is light, about 5 minutes. Whisk the warm milk mixture into the egg-and-sugar mixture until it has all been incorporated. Whisk in the dry mixture until it has been incorporated.

7. Divide the batter between prepared pans and place them in the oven. Bake until the tops are light brown and a toothpick inserted into the center of each cake comes out clean, about 20 minutes. Remove the pans from the oven and let cool completely, about 2 hours.

8. After 2 hours, invert the cakes onto wire racks and remove the parchment paper. Remove the filling from the refrigerator and whisk to loosen it slightly. Spoon the filling onto the top of one of the cakes and spread it evenly over the surface. Place the second cake, flat-side up, on top of the filling.

9. Whisk the frosting to loosen and then spread it over the top of the cake. Place the cake in the refrigerator for at least 3 hours before serving.

YIELD: **8 SERVINGS**

ACTIVE TIME: **45 MINUTES**

TOTAL TIME: **24 HOURS**

Crack Pie

INGREDIENTS

FOR THE CRUST

1 STICK UNSALTED BUTTER, AT ROOM TEMPERATURE

⅓ CUP GENTLY PACKED LIGHT BROWN SUGAR

2 TABLESPOONS GRANULATED SUGAR

1 LARGE EGG, AT ROOM TEMPERATURE

¾ CUP OATS, PLUS 2 TABLESPOONS

½ CUP ALL-PURPOSE FLOUR

⅛ TEASPOON BAKING POWDER

⅛ TEASPOON BAKING SODA

¼ TEASPOON KOSHER SALT

FOR THE FILLING

¾ CUP GRANULATED SUGAR

½ CUP GENTLY PACKED LIGHT BROWN SUGAR

1 TABLESPOON NONFAT MILK POWDER

¼ TEASPOON KOSHER SALT

1 STICK UNSALTED BUTTER, MELTED AND SLIGHTLY COOLED

Continued...

DIRECTIONS

1. Preheat the oven to 350°F and line a 9 x 13-inch baking sheet with parchment paper. To begin preparations for the crust, place 5 tablespoons of the butter, ¼ cup of the brown sugar, and the granulated sugar in a mixing bowl and beat with a handheld mixer until pale and fluffy. Add the egg, beat to incorporate, and then stir in the ¾ cup of oats, flour, baking powder, baking soda, and salt. Press the mixture into the baking sheet, place it in the oven, and bake for 16 to 18 minutes, until it is dry to the touch. Remove and let cool completely.

2. When the crust has cooled, break it up into pieces, place them in a food processor and pulse until they are fine crumbs. Add the remaining butter, brown sugar, and oats and pulse until incorporated. Grease a 9-inch pie plate with nonstick cooking spray and press the mixture into it. Place the crust in the refrigerator.

3. To begin preparations for the filling, place the sugars, milk powder, and salt in a mixing bowl and stir to combine. Add the melted butter and beat with a handheld mixer until pale and fluffy. Add the cream, egg yolks, and vanilla and beat until thoroughly combined.

Continued...

½ CUP HEAVY CREAM

4 LARGE EGG YOLKS

1 TEASPOON PURE VANILLA EXTRACT

¼ CUP CONFECTIONERS' SUGAR

4. Pour the filling into the piecrust, place the pie in the oven, and bake for 30 minutes. Reduce the oven temperature to 325°F and bake for another 20 minutes, until the filling is set and the center wobbles slightly when poked. Remove from the oven, let cool completely, cover with plastic wrap, and chill overnight. When ready to serve, sprinkle the confectioners' sugar over the top.

YIELD: **8 SERVINGS**

ACTIVE TIME: **15 MINUTES**

TOTAL TIME: **1 HOUR AND 15 MINUTES**

Shoo-Fly Pie

INGREDIENTS

1 CUP MOLASSES

1 TEASPOON BAKING SODA

¾ CUP BOILING WATER

1 SWEET CRUST (SEE PAGE 13)

1½ CUPS ALL-PURPOSE FLOUR

½ CUP GENTLY PACKED DARK BROWN SUGAR

½ TEASPOON CINNAMON

PINCH OF GRATED FRESH NUTMEG

PINCH OF KOSHER SALT

1 STICK UNSALTED BUTTER, CHILLED AND DIVIDED INTO TABLESPOONS

DIRECTIONS

1. Preheat the oven to 350°F. Place the molasses, baking soda, and boiling water in a large mixing bowl and stir to combine. Evenly distribute the mixture in the piecrust.

2. Place the flour, brown sugar, cinnamon, nutmeg, and salt in a large mixing bowl and stir to combine. Add the butter and work the mixture with your hands until it is sticking together in clumps. Distribute the mixture over the pie.

3. Place the pie in the oven and bake for about 45 minutes, until the crust is golden brown and the topping is dry to the touch. Remove from the oven and let cool before serving.

YIELD: **8 SERVINGS**

ACTIVE TIME: **15 MINUTES**

TOTAL TIME: **1 HOUR AND 45 MINUTES**

Mississippi Mud Pie

INGREDIENTS

1½ STICKS UNSALTED BUTTER

1 CUP GENTLY PACKED DARK BROWN SUGAR

4 LARGE EGGS, LIGHTLY BEATEN

¼ CUP UNSWEETENED COCOA POWDER

1¼ CUPS BITTERSWEET CHOCOLATE CHIPS, MELTED AND SLIGHTLY COOLED

2 TEASPOONS INSTANT COFFEE GROUNDS

1¼ CUPS HEAVY CREAM

1 COCOA CRUST (SEE PAGE 17)

WHIPPED CREAM (SEE PAGE 38), AS NEEDED

BITTERSWEET CHOCOLATE, GRATED, FOR GARNISH

DIRECTIONS

1. Preheat the oven to 350°F. Place the butter and brown sugar in a mixing bowl and beat with a handheld mixer until pale and fluffy. Add the eggs and cocoa powder, beat to incorporate, and then fold in the chocolate chips and coffee. Add the cream and beat to incorporate.

2. Evenly distribute the mixture in the piecrust, place the pie in the oven, and bake for about 35 minutes, until the filling is set. Remove from the oven and let the pie cool completely. Top with the Whipped Cream and shaved chocolate before serving.

Rhubarb, Brown Sugar & Fennel Pie

YIELD: **8 SERVINGS**

ACTIVE TIME: **25 MINUTES**

TOTAL TIME: **1 HOUR AND 45 MINUTES**

INGREDIENTS

2 PERFECT PIECRUSTS (SEE PAGE 10)

3 CUPS SLICED RHUBARB

1 FENNEL BULB, TRIMMED AND CHOPPED

⅔ CUP PACKED LIGHT BROWN SUGAR

JUICE OF 1 ORANGE

1 TEASPOON PURE VANILLA EXTRACT

2 TABLESPOONS PASTIS (OPTIONAL)

¼ CUP WATER

2 TABLESPOONS CORNSTARCH

2 TABLESPOONS MILK

1 TO 2 TEASPOONS FENNEL SEEDS

DIRECTIONS

1. Grease a 9-inch pie plate with nonstick cooking spray and place one of the piecrusts in it.

2. Place the rhubarb, chopped fennel, brown sugar, orange juice, vanilla, pastis (if using), and ¼ cup water in a saucepan, partially cover, and cook over medium heat until the rhubarb is very tender and juicy, 12 to 15 minutes. Remove from heat, stir in the cornstarch, and let the mixture cool. Preheat the oven to 350°F.

3. Evenly distribute the rhubarb mixture in the piecrust, top with the remaining piecrust, and crimp the edge to seal. Cut four or five slits in the top crust, brush it with the milk, and sprinkle the fennel seeds on top.

4. Place the pie in the oven and bake for about 45 minutes, until the top crust is golden brown and the filling is bubbling. Remove from the oven and let cool before serving.

CHAPTER 5

HANDPIES

Though far from being considered canonical, the handpie has its own healthy legion of fans. This outpouring of love seems tied to the handpie's ability to capitalize on a phenomenon storytellers have successfully mined for years: that an unassuming exterior is often hiding something unique and lovely.

The prospect that something seemingly ordinary could contain some glorious surprise is always tempting, and these handpies—whether sweet or savory—pay off on that promise.

YIELD: **6 SERVINGS**

ACTIVE TIME: **15 MINUTES**

TOTAL TIME: **1 HOUR**

Whoopie Pies

INGREDIENTS

2½ STICKS UNSALTED BUTTER, AT ROOM TEMPERATURE

1¼ CUPS CONFECTIONERS' SUGAR

2 PINCHES OF KOSHER SALT

2½ TEASPOONS PURE VANILLA EXTRACT

2½ CUPS MARSHMALLOW CRÈME

2 CUPS ALL-PURPOSE FLOUR

½ CUP UNSWEETENED COCOA POWDER

1 TEASPOON BAKING SODA

1 CUP GENTLY PACKED LIGHT BROWN SUGAR

1 LARGE EGG, AT ROOM TEMPERATURE

1 CUP BUTTERMILK

DIRECTIONS

1. Place 12 tablespoons of the butter and the confectioners' sugar in a mixing bowl and beat until the mixture is fluffy. Add a pinch of salt and 1½ teaspoons of the vanilla and beat until combined. Add the marshmallow crème and beat until incorporated. Place the filling in the refrigerator and chill for at least 30 minutes.

2. Preheat the oven to 350°F.

3. Place the flour, cocoa powder, baking soda, and the remaining salt in a bowl and whisk to combine. Place the remaining butter and the brown sugar in another mixing bowl and beat until the mixture is fluffy. Add the egg, beat until incorporated, and then add the remaining vanilla. Gradually add the dry mixture and the buttermilk, alternating between them. Beat until incorporated and then scoop the batter onto parchment-lined baking sheets, making sure to leave plenty of room between the scoops.

4. Place the sheets in the oven and bake, while rotating and switching their positions halfway through, for 15 minutes. The cakes should feel springy to the touch when done. Remove from the oven and let cool on the baking sheets.

5. Place some filling in the center of one cake, top with another cake, and press down to spread the filling to the edges. Repeat with the remaining filling and cakes and then serve.

CRÈME OF THE CROP

Marshmallow crème is a marshmallow confectionary spread, the best-known version of which is Marshmallow Fluff. Fluff was invented by Archibald Query in Somerville, Mass., near the turn of the 20th century. After selling his creation door-to-door for a time, Query sold it to two candy makers in nearby Lynn, H. Allen Durkee and Fred Mower, for $500 in 1920. Durkee and Mower's version (originally called Toot Sweet Marshmallow Fluff) hit the market in 1917, and it remains a pantry staple throughout the Northeast, where the whoopie pie and the Fluffernutter sandwich remain regional favorites.

Marshmallow crème is also a traditional part of Middle Eastern cuisine. While this iteration, which is known as *natef*, was mentioned in a 10th-century cookbook, modern commercial varieties are practically identical to those produced in the U.S.

YIELD: **12 SERVINGS**

ACTIVE TIME: **20 MINUTES**

TOTAL TIME: **1 HOUR**

Squash Whoopie Pies

INGREDIENTS

1⅓ CUPS ALL-PURPOSE FLOUR

1 TEASPOON CINNAMON

1 TEASPOON GROUND GINGER

¼ TEASPOON GROUND CLOVES

½ TEASPOON GRATED FRESH NUTMEG

½ TEASPOON BAKING SODA

½ TEASPOON BAKING POWDER

1 TEASPOON KOSHER SALT

1 CUP GENTLY PACKED LIGHT BROWN SUGAR

2 TABLESPOONS REAL MAPLE SYRUP

1 CUP PUREED BUTTERNUT OR ACORN SQUASH

1 EGG

1 CUP VEGETABLE OIL

1⅓ CUPS CONFECTIONERS' SUGAR

4 TABLESPOONS UNSALTED BUTTER

½ LB. CREAM CHEESE, AT ROOM TEMPERATURE

1-INCH PIECE OF FRESH GINGER, PEELED AND GRATED

½ TEASPOON PURE VANILLA EXTRACT

DIRECTIONS

1. Preheat the oven to 350°F. Sift the flour, cinnamon, ground ginger, cloves, nutmeg, baking soda, baking powder, and salt into a mixing bowl.
2. Place the brown sugar, maple syrup, pureed squash, egg, and vegetable oil in a separate mixing bowl and stir until combined. Sift the dry mixture into the squash mixture and stir until it has been incorporated.
3. Use an ice cream scoop to place dollops of the batter onto parchment-lined baking sheets. Make sure to leave plenty of space between the scoops. Place the sheets in the oven and bake until the cakes are golden brown, about 10 to 15 minutes. Remove and let cool.
4. While the squash cakes are cooling, place the remaining ingredients in a bowl and beat with a handheld mixer until the mixture is fluffy.
5. When the cakes have cooled completely, spread the filling on one of the cakes. Top with another cake and repeat until all of the cakes and filling have been used.

Chocolate Raspberry Whoopie Pies

YIELD: **14 SERVINGS**

ACTIVE TIME: **15 MINUTES**

TOTAL TIME: **1 HOUR**

INGREDIENTS

FOR THE DOUGH

1 STICK UNSALTED BUTTER, AT ROOM TEMPERATURE

½ CUP SUGAR

1 LARGE EGG

1 TEASPOON PURE VANILLA EXTRACT

1½ CUPS SIFTED ALL-PURPOSE FLOUR

1 TEASPOON BAKING POWDER

⅔ CUP MILK

⅓ CUP UNSWEETENED COCOA POWDER

⅓ CUP ALMOND MEAL

FOR THE FILLING

¾ CUP RASPBERRIES

1 STICK UNSALTED BUTTER, AT ROOM TEMPERATURE

¼ CUP GRANULATED SUGAR

½ CUP CREAM CHEESE, AT ROOM TEMPERATURE

1 CUP SIFTED CONFECTIONERS' SUGAR

DIRECTIONS

1. Preheat the oven to 350°F and line two baking sheets with parchment paper. To begin preparations for the dough, place the butter and sugar in a mixing bowl and beat with a handheld mixer until light and fluffy. Incorporate the egg and vanilla and then gradually incorporate the flour and baking powder, making sure each addition has been thoroughly incorporated before adding the next portion. Add the milk, cocoa powder, and almond meal and stir until the batter is smooth.

2. Scoop 28 mounds of the batter onto the baking sheets, making sure to leave plenty of room between the mounds. Place in the oven and bake for about 15 minutes, until the cakes are slightly puffy and dry to the touch. Remove from the oven and let cool completely.

3. To prepare the filling, place the raspberries in a food processor and puree. Place the butter and granulated sugar in a mixing bowl and beat with a handheld mixer until lightly and fluffy. Add the cream cheese, beat until thoroughly combined, and then stir in the raspberry puree. Gradually incorporate the confectioners' sugar until the desired consistency has been achieved. Spread the mixture on half of the cakes and then place then remaining cakes on top to assemble the whoopie pies.

Roasted Strawberry Handpies

YIELD: **8 SERVINGS**

ACTIVE TIME: **40 MINUTES**

TOTAL TIME: **2 HOURS**

INGREDIENTS

3 QUARTS FRESH STRAWBERRIES, HULLED AND SLICED

1 CUP GRANULATED SUGAR

2 TEASPOONS FRESH LEMON JUICE

1 TABLESPOON CORNSTARCH

1½ TEASPOONS WATER

1 BALL OF PERFECT PIECRUST DOUGH (SEE PAGE 10)

2 EGGS, BEATEN

1½ CUPS SIFTED CONFECTIONERS' SUGAR

3 TO 4 TABLESPOONS WHOLE MILK

1 TEASPOON CINNAMON

DIRECTIONS

1. Preheat the oven to 400°F.

2. Place the strawberries on a baking sheet and roast in the oven until they start to darken and release their juice, about 20 to 30 minutes. If you prefer, you can roast them for up to an hour. Cooking the strawberries for longer will caramelize the sugars and lend them an even richer flavor.

3. Remove the strawberries from the oven and place them in a saucepan with the granulated sugar and lemon juice. Bring to a simmer over medium heat and cook for 20 minutes, until the mixture has thickened slightly.

4. Place the cornstarch and water in a small cup and stir until there are no lumps in the mixture. Add the slurry to the saucepan and stir until the mixture is syrupy. Remove the pan from heat.

5. Divide the ball of piecrust dough into two squares and then cut each square into quarters. Spoon some of the strawberry mixture into the center of each quarter.

6. Take a bottom corner of each pie and fold to the opposite top corner. Press down to ensure that none of the mixture leaks out and then use a fork to seal the edge. Place the pies on a baking sheet and brush them with the beaten egg. Place in the oven and bake until golden brown, about 20 to 30 minutes.

7. While the pies are cooking, place the confectioners' sugar, milk, and cinnamon in a bowl and stir until well combined.

8. Remove the pies from the oven, brush them with the sugar-and-cinnamon glaze, and let cool before serving.

YIELD: **12 SERVINGS**

ACTIVE TIME: **45 MINUTES**

TOTAL TIME: **5 HOURS**

Pot Roast Handpies

INGREDIENTS

2 LBS. BOTTOM ROUND ROAST

SALT AND PEPPER, TO TASTE

1 CUP ALL-PURPOSE FLOUR, PLUS ¼ CUP

3 TABLESPOONS OLIVE OIL

2 LBS. CARROTS, PEELED AND LEFT WHOLE

8 SHALLOTS, PEELED AND LEFT WHOLE

2 TO 3 BAY LEAVES

8 TO 10 SPRIGS OF FRESH THYME

¼ CUP WORCESTERSHIRE SAUCE

1 CUP WATER

2 CUPS BEEF STOCK

¾ LB. FROZEN GREEN PEAS

2 BALLS OF PERFECT PIECRUSTS DOUGH (SEE PAGE 10)

1 EGG YOLK

1 TABLESPOON HEAVY CREAM

DIRECTIONS

1. Preheat the oven to 450°F. Rinse and pat the roast dry. Season all over with salt and pepper and then sprinkle the 1 cup of flour over the roast.

2. Place the oil in a Dutch oven and warm over medium-high heat. When the oil starts to shimmer, place the roast in the pot and sear until it is browned all over, 6 to 8 minutes. Remove the roast from the pan, place the carrots in the Dutch oven, and place the roast on top of the carrots. Add the shallots, bay leaves, thyme, Worcestershire sauce, and water. Cover the Dutch oven, place it in the oven, and cook for 1 hour.

3. Reduce the oven's temperature to 350°F and cook for another hour. After 1 hour, combine the remaining flour and the beef stock. Strain the mixture over the roast, return the roast to the oven, and cook for about 1 hour, until it is very tender. Remove everything but the liquid from the Dutch oven. Cook the liquid over medium-high heat until it has reduced to the desired consistency. Season with salt and pepper, remove from heat, and let cool.

4. Roll the balls of dough out and cut them into 12 circles. Chop the meat, carrots, and shallots and add them to the gravy along with the frozen peas. Preheat the oven to 375°F.

5. Place ⅓ cup of the filling in the center of each circle. Fold into a half-moons and crimp the edges to seal. Cut a few slits in the top of each handpie.

6. Place the egg yolk and cream in a small bowl, stir to combine, and brush the handpies with the egg wash. Place the handpies on a baking sheet, place them in the oven, and bake for about 30 minutes, until golden brown. Remove and let cool slightly before serving.

YIELD: **4 SERVINGS**

ACTIVE TIME: **30 MINUTES**

TOTAL TIME: **2 HOURS AND 30 MINUTES**

Runzas

INGREDIENTS

FOR THE DOUGH

¾ CUP LUKEWARM WATER (90°F)

1 TEASPOON ACTIVE DRY YEAST

½ CUP SWEETENED CONDENSED MILK

¼ CUP VEGETABLE OIL

2 TABLESPOONS SUGAR

1 LARGE EGG

3½ CUPS ALL-PURPOSE FLOUR, PLUS MORE FOR DUSTING

1 TEASPOON KOSHER SALT

FOR THE FILLING

6 TABLESPOONS UNSALTED BUTTER

1½ LBS. GROUND BEEF

1 YELLOW ONION, MINCED

2½ CUPS CHOPPED GREEN CABBAGE

SALT AND PEPPER, TO TASTE

FOR SERVING

SAUERKRAUT

DIRECTIONS

1. To prepare the dough, place the water and yeast in the mixing bowl of a stand mixer and let it stand until it is foamy, about 5 minutes. Fit a stand mixer with the dough hook attachment, add the remaining ingredients, and mix on low speed until the dough holds together. Increase the speed to medium and mix until the dough is a ball and no longer sticks to the side of the mixing bowl. Cover with a damp cloth and let rest until it doubles in size, about 1 hour.

2. To prepare the filling, place 1 tablespoon of the butter in a large skillet and melt over medium-high heat. Add the ground beef and cook, while using a fork to break it up, until it is browned, about 6 minutes. Place the meat on a paper towel-lined plate to drain, wipe out the skillet, and add another tablespoon of butter. Melt over medium heat, add the onion, and cook until it has softened, about 5 minutes. Add the cabbage and cook until it starts to wilt. Return the meat to the pan, stir to combine, and season with salt and pepper. Let the mixture cool.

3. Place the dough on a flour-dusted work surface, cut it into eight pieces, and roll each one into a 6-inch circle. Place about ¾ cup of the cooled filling in the center of a circle, fold the dough over it, and crimp to seal. Place the handpies on a parchment-lined baking sheet, cover with plastic wrap, and let them rise for 30 minutes.

4. Preheat the oven to 350°F. Place the handpies in the oven and cook for 10 minutes. Melt the remaining butter in a skillet and set it aside. After 10 minutes, remove the baking sheet from the oven and brush the top of each handpie with some of the melted butter. Return to the oven and bake until golden brown, about 10 minutes. Remove, brush with any remaining butter, and serve with sauerkraut.

YIELD: **6 SERVINGS**

ACTIVE TIME: **30 MINUTES**

TOTAL TIME: **1 HOUR AND 15 MINUTES**

Cornish Pasties

INGREDIENTS

FOR THE DOUGH

3 CUPS ALL-PURPOSE FLOUR, PLUS MORE AS NEEDED

¾ TEASPOON KOSHER SALT

½ CUP LARD OR UNSALTED BUTTER, CUT INTO SMALL PIECES

1 LARGE EGG, BEATEN

¼ CUP COLD WATER, PLUS MORE AS NEEDED

2 TEASPOONS DISTILLED WHITE VINEGAR

FOR THE FILLING

¾ LB. SKIRT STEAK, CUT INTO ½-INCH CUBES

¼ CUP PEELED AND CHOPPED PARSNIPS

¼ CUP PEELED AND CHOPPED TURNIPS

1 SMALL ONION, CHOPPED

1 CUP PEELED AND CHOPPED POTATO

1 TABLESPOON FINELY CHOPPED FRESH THYME

2 TABLESPOONS TOMATO PASTE

SALT AND PEPPER, TO TASTE

1 LARGE EGG, BEATEN

1 TABLESPOON WATER

DIRECTIONS

1. To prepare the dough, place the flour and salt in a bowl, add the lard or butter, and use a pastry blender to work the mixture until it is coarse crumbs. Beat the egg, water, and vinegar together in a separate bowl and then drizzle this mixture over the flour mixture. Use the pastry blender to work the mixture until it starts to hold together. Knead the dough with your hands, adding more water in 1-teaspoon increments if it is too dry. Cut the dough into 6 pieces, cover with plastic wrap, and chill in the refrigerator.

2. Preheat the oven to 400°F and prepare the filling. Place all of the ingredients, except for the egg and water, in a bowl and stir to combine. Place the egg and water in a separate bowl and beat to combine.

3. Place the pieces of dough on a flour-dusted work surface, roll each one into an 8-inch circle, and place ½ cup of the filling in the center of each circle. Brush the edge of each circle with water, fold each one into a half-moon, and crimp the edge to seal. Place the sealed handpies on a parchment-lined baking sheet.

4. Place the egg and water in a small bowl and beat to combine. Brush the pastries with the egg wash and use a paring knife to make a small incision in the side of each one. Bake in the oven for 15 minutes, reduce the temperature to 350°F, and bake for another 25 minutes. Remove from oven and let cool on a wire rack before serving.

YIELD: **4 SERVINGS**

ACTIVE TIME: **30 MINUTES**

TOTAL TIME: **1 HOUR AND 45 MINUTES**

Empanadas

INGREDIENTS

FOR THE DOUGH

¼ TEASPOON KOSHER SALT

6 TABLESPOONS WARM WATER (110°F)

1½ CUPS ALL-PURPOSE FLOUR, PLUS MORE AS NEEDED

3 TABLESPOONS LARD OR UNSALTED BUTTER, CUT INTO SMALL PIECES

FOR THE FILLING

2 TEASPOONS VEGETABLE OIL, PLUS MORE AS NEEDED

1 YELLOW ONION, MINCED

1 GARLIC CLOVE, MINCED

¾ LB. GROUND PORK

1 (14 OZ.) CAN OF CRUSHED TOMATOES

½ TEASPOON KOSHER SALT

¼ TEASPOON BLACK PEPPER

1 CINNAMON STICK

2 WHOLE CLOVES

2 TABLESPOONS RAISINS

2 TEASPOONS APPLE CIDER VINEGAR

2 TABLESPOONS SLIVERED ALMONDS, TOASTED

DIRECTIONS

1. To prepare the dough, dissolve the salt in the warm water. Place the flour in a mixing bowl, add the lard or butter, and work the mixture with a pastry blender until it is coarse crumbs. Add the salted water and knead the mixture until a stiff dough forms. Cut the dough into eight pieces, cover them with plastic wrap, and chill in the refrigerator for 20 minutes.

2. To prepare the filling, place the vegetable oil in a skillet and warm over medium heat. Add the onion and cook until it has softened, about 5 minutes. Add the garlic, cook for 2 minutes, and then add the ground pork. Cook, while breaking it up with a fork, until light brown, about 5 minutes. Drain off any excess fat and add the tomatoes, salt, pepper, cinnamon stick, cloves, raisins, and vinegar. Simmer until the filling is thick, about 30 minutes. Remove from heat and let cool before folding in the toasted almonds.

3. Add vegetable oil to a Dutch oven until it is 2 inches deep and bring it to 350°F. Preheat the oven to 200°F and place a platter in the oven. Place the pieces of dough on a flour-dusted work surface and roll each one into a 5-inch circle. Place 3 tablespoons of the filling in the center of one circle, brush the edge with water, and fold into a half-moon. Press down on the edge to seal the empanada tight, trying to remove as much air as possible. Repeat with the remaining filling and pieces of dough.

4. Working in two batches, place the empanadas in the hot oil and fry until golden brown, about 5 minutes. Drain the cooked empanadas on paper towels and place them in the warm oven while you cook the next batch.

YIELD: **4 SERVINGS**

ACTIVE TIME: **30 MINUTES**

TOTAL TIME: **1 HOUR AND 45 MINUTES**

Vegetarian Empanadas

INGREDIENTS

2 TEASPOONS VEGETABLE OIL, PLUS MORE AS NEEDED

1 YELLOW ONION, MINCED

1 CUP SHREDDED NAPA CABBAGE

2 CARROTS, PEELED AND GRATED

1 GARLIC CLOVE, MINCED

1 (14 OZ.) CAN OF DICED TOMATOES

½ TEASPOON KOSHER SALT

¼ TEASPOON BLACK PEPPER

½ TEASPOON ACHIOTE

½ TEASPOON CUMIN

CHILI POWDER, TO TASTE

DOUGH FROM EMPANADAS (SEE PAGE 183, MADE WITH BUTTER)

DIRECTIONS

1. Place the vegetable oil in a skillet and warm over medium heat. Add the onion, cabbage, and carrots and cook until they are soft, about 10 minutes. Add the garlic, cook for 2 minutes, and then transfer the mixture to a mixing bowl. Add the tomatoes and seasonings, stir to combine, and let the mixture cool completely.

2. Add vegetable oil to a Dutch oven until it is 2 inches deep and bring it to 350°F. Preheat the oven to 200°F and place a platter in the oven. Place the pieces of dough on a flour-dusted work surface and roll each one into a 5-inch circle. Place 3 tablespoons of the filling in the center of a circle, brush the edge with water, and fold into a half-moon. Press down on the edge to seal the empanada tight, trying to remove as much air as possible. Repeat with the remaining filling and pieces of dough.

3. Working in two batches, place the empanadas in the hot oil and fry until golden brown, about 5 minutes. Drain the cooked empanadas on paper towels and place them in the warm oven while you cook the next batch.

NOTE: Achiote is a vibrant orange-red spice that is made from ground annatto seeds, and its nutty, sweet, and earthy flavor is the key to these delectable pockets.

Classic Meat Pies

YIELD: **4 SERVINGS**

ACTIVE TIME: **30 MINUTES**

TOTAL TIME: **1 HOUR AND 30 MINUTES**

INGREDIENTS

2 TABLESPOONS UNSALTED BUTTER

1 LARGE YELLOW ONION, MINCED

½ SMALL RUTABAGA, PEELED AND DICED

1 TEASPOON KOSHER SALT, PLUS A PINCH

2 LBS. GROUND BEEF

1 TEASPOON DRIED THYME

1 TEASPOON DRIED SAGE

½ TEASPOON BLACK PEPPER

2 BALLS OF PERFECT PIECRUSTS DOUGH (SEE PAGE 10)

ALL-PURPOSE FLOUR, AS NEEDED

1 LARGE EGG

1 TABLESPOON WATER

DIRECTIONS

1. Preheat the oven to 375°F. Place the butter in a Dutch oven and melt over medium heat. Add the onion, rutabaga, and the pinch of salt and cook until the onion and rutabaga have softened, about 6 minutes. Add the ground beef, raise the heat to medium-high, and cook, while breaking up the beef with a fork, until browned, about 8 minutes. Add the remaining salt, thyme, sage, and pepper, stir to incorporate, and then drain the mixture to remove any excess liquid.

2. Place the balls of dough on a flour-dusted work surface and divide them into eight pieces. Roll four of the pieces into 4- or 5-inch circles. Roll the other pieces into 3-inch circles. Place the larger pieces of dough in individual ramekins or small pie plates that have been greased with nonstick cooking spray. Spoon the ground beef mixture into each crust, place a smaller piece of dough on top of each pie, and crimp the edge to seal.

3. Place the egg and water in a small bowl, stir to combine, and brush each of the pies with the egg wash. Make a few slits in the top of each pie, place them in the oven, and bake for about 45 minutes, until the tops are golden brown. Remove from the oven and let the pies cool before serving.

YIELD: **8 SERVINGS**

ACTIVE TIME: **20 MINUTES**

TOTAL TIME: **1 HOUR AND 10 MINUTES**

Mushroom Handpies

INGREDIENTS

3 TABLESPOONS OLIVE OIL

6 CUPS MIXED WILD MUSHROOMS, CLEANED AND CHOPPED

1 GARLIC CLOVE, MINCED

½ CUP GRATED PARMESAN CHEESE

1 TABLESPOON FINELY CHOPPED FRESH THYME

1 TABLESPOON FRESH LEMON JUICE

½ TEASPOON KOSHER SALT

¼ TEASPOON BLACK PEPPER

2 BALLS OF PERFECT PIECRUSTS DOUGH (SEE PAGE 10)

ALL-PURPOSE FLOUR, AS NEEDED

1 LARGE EGG, BEATEN

1 TABLESPOON WATER

DIRECTIONS

1. Preheat the oven to 350°F. Place the oil in a large Dutch oven and warm over medium heat. When the oil starts to shimmer, add the mushrooms and cook, stirring occasionally, until they release their liquid and start to brown, about 8 minutes. Add the garlic and cook until fragrant, about 1 minute.

2. Drain the mixture, pressing down to remove as much liquid from the mushrooms as possible. Transfer to a mixing bowl, add the Parmesan, thyme, lemon juice, salt, and pepper and stir to combine.

3. Place the balls of dough on a flour-dusted work surface and roll them out to ¼ inch thick. Cut eight 3-inch circles out of each piece of dough and place half of them on a parchment-lined baking sheet. Spoon the mushroom filling into the centers of the rounds on the baking sheet. Place the other pieces of dough on top and crimp the edges to seal.

4. Cut a few slits in the top of each handpie. Place the egg and water in a small bowl, stir to combine, and brush the handpies with the egg wash. Place the handpies in the oven and bake for about 35 minutes, until golden brown. Remove from the oven and let cool briefly before serving.

CHAPTER 6

SAVORY

Just because it is deserving of the dessert crown doesn't mean that the pie is limited to sweet fillings. Rest assured, this versatile container has the ability to accommodate almost any flavor one can throw at it.

From quiches you can proudly place on the table at a potluck brunch to filo-encased delicacies that are impossibly light and crunchy, this collection of pies shows that while the savory is outnumbered by the sweet in the pie universe, that asymmetry has nothing to do with deliciousness.

YIELD: **8 SERVINGS**

ACTIVE TIME: **15 MINUTES**

TOTAL TIME: **1 HOUR AND 40 MINUTES**

Salmon & Dill Quiche

INGREDIENTS

1 TEASPOON DIJON MUSTARD

1 PERFECT PIECRUST, BLIND BAKED (SEE PAGES 10–11)

1 LB. SMOKED SALMON, TORN INTO BITE-SIZED PIECES

4 EGGS

1 CUP HALF-AND-HALF

1 TEASPOON KOSHER SALT

½ TEASPOON BLACK PEPPER

1 TABLESPOON FINELY CHOPPED FRESH DILL

½ CUP CREAM CHEESE, AT ROOM TEMPERATURE

DIRECTIONS

1. Preheat the oven to 350°F. Brush the mustard over the bottom of the piecrust. Distribute the salmon pieces over the crust and set it aside.

2. Place the eggs, half-and-half, salt, and pepper in a mixing bowl and stir until combined. Stir in the dill, pour the egg mixture over the salmon, and shake the pie plate to evenly distribute the liquid.

3. Dot the mixture with spoonfuls of the cream cheese, place the quiche in the oven, and bake for about 35 minutes, until it is puffy and golden brown. Remove from the oven and let cool for 10 minutes before serving.

Quiche Lorraine

YIELD: **8 SERVINGS**

ACTIVE TIME: **15 MINUTES**

TOTAL TIME: **1 HOUR AND 30 MINUTES**

INGREDIENTS

8 SLICES OF BACON, COOKED AND CHOPPED

1 PERFECT PIECRUST, BLIND BAKED (SEE PAGES 10–11)

½ CUP MILK

½ CUP HEAVY CREAM

4 LARGE EGGS

⅛ TEASPOON KOSHER SALT

PINCH OF GRATED FRESH NUTMEG

½ CUP GRATED GRUYÈRE CHEESE

DIRECTIONS

1. Preheat the oven to 350°F. Sprinkle the bacon over the piecrust and set it aside.
2. Place the milk, cream, eggs, salt, and nutmeg in a mixing bowl and whisk until thoroughly combined. Pour the mixture into the crust and gently shake the pie plate to evenly distribute.
3. Sprinkle the Gruyère on top, place the quiche in the oven, and bake for about 30 minutes, until the filling is just set. Remove and let cool for 10 minutes before serving.

YIELD: **8 SERVINGS**

ACTIVE TIME: **25 MINUTES**

TOTAL TIME: **2 HOURS**

Bacon & Zucchini Quiche

INGREDIENTS

8 SLICES THICK-CUT BACON, COOKED AND CHOPPED

1 PERFECT PIECRUST, BLIND BAKED (SEE PAGES 10–11)

1 TABLESPOON OLIVE OIL

1 SMALL ZUCCHINI, TRIMMED AND SLICED INTO THIN ROUNDS

1 GARLIC CLOVE, MINCED

4 OZ. GARLIC & HERB GOAT CHEESE

4 EGGS

1 CUP HALF-AND-HALF

½ TEASPOON KOSHER SALT

½ TEASPOON BLACK PEPPER

DIRECTIONS

1. Preheat the oven to 350°F. Sprinkle the bacon over the crust and set aside.

2. Place the olive oil in a skillet and warm over medium-high heat. When the oil starts to shimmer, add the zucchini and cook until it has softened, about 10 minutes. Add the garlic and cook for another minute. Spoon the mixture over the bacon in the piecrust. Dot the mixture with the goat cheese and set aside.

3. Place the eggs, half-and-half, salt, and pepper in a mixing bowl and whisk to combine. Pour the egg mixture into the piecrust and gently shake the pie plate to distribute evenly.

4. Place the quiche in the oven and bake for 35 minutes, until the quiche is puffy and golden brown. Remove from the oven and let cool for 10 minutes before serving.

Fennel, Pepper & Hazelnut Quiche

YIELD: **8 SERVINGS**

ACTIVE TIME: **20 MINUTES**

TOTAL TIME: **1 HOUR AND 45 MINUTES**

INGREDIENTS

2 LARGE RED BELL PEPPERS, STEMMED AND SEEDED

4 LARGE EGGS

2 LARGE EGG YOLKS

1 CUP CRÈME FRAÎCHE (SEE SIDEBAR)

1 CUP MILK

1 CUP GRATED CHEDDAR OR GRUYÈRE CHEESE

½ TEASPOON KOSHER SALT

¼ TEASPOON BLACK PEPPER

1 PERFECT PIECRUST, BLIND BAKED (SEE PAGES 10–11)

6 FENNEL BULBS, TRIMMED AND CHOPPED

¼ CUP CHOPPED HAZELNUTS, FOR GARNISH

2 TABLESPOONS FINELY CHOPPED FRESH CHIVES, FOR GARNISH

DIRECTIONS

1. Preheat the oven to 350°F. Bring water to a boil in a large saucepan and prepare an ice water bath. Place the peppers in the boiling water for 15 seconds, transfer them to the ice water bath, and let them sit for 2 minutes. Peel the peppers and cut each one into five or six pieces.

2. Place the eggs, egg yolks, crème fraîche, milk, cheese, salt, and pepper in a mixing bowl and stir until thoroughly combined. Pour the mixture into the piecrust, shake the pie plate gently, and evenly distribute the peppers and the fennel over the quiche.

3. Place the quiche in the oven and bake for about 35 minutes, until it is puffy and golden brown. Remove from the oven and let cool for 10 minutes. Garnish with the hazelnuts and chives before serving.

CRÈME FRAÎCHE

You can find crème fraîche at the store, but as it is typically expensive and very easy to make at home, it's better to handle it yourself. Simply combine 1 cup heavy cream and 1 tablespoon of buttermilk in a mason jar, cover it, and let stand at room temperature for 12 hours. Use immediately or store in the refrigerator for up to 1 month.

YIELD: **8 SERVINGS**

ACTIVE TIME: **20 MINUTES**

TOTAL TIME: **2 HOURS**

Springtime Quiche

INGREDIENTS

2 CUPS CHOPPED ASPARAGUS

1 PERFECT PIECRUST, BLIND BAKED (SEE PAGES 10–11)

6 LARGE EGGS

2 LARGE EGG YOLKS

1 CUP CRÈME FRAÎCHE (SEE PAGE 199 FOR HOMEMADE)

½ CUP MILK

½ CUP HEAVY CREAM

1 CUP GRATED CHEDDAR CHEESE

½ TEASPOON KOSHER SALT

¼ TEASPOON BLACK PEPPER

½ CUP FROZEN PEAS

2 TABLESPOONS FRESH MINT LEAVES, FOR GARNISH

DIRECTIONS

1. Preheat the oven to 350°F. Bring water to a boil in a large saucepan and prepare an ice water bath. Place the asparagus in the boiling water for 15 seconds, transfer to the ice water bath, and let it sit for 2 minutes. Drain, pat the asparagus dry, and distribute the pieces in the piecrust.

2. Place the eggs, egg yolks, crème fraîche, milk, cream, cheese, salt, and pepper in a mixing bowl, stir to combine, and then stir in the peas. Pour the mixture into the crust and gently shake the pie plate to distribute evenly.

3. Place the quiche in the oven and bake until it is puffy and golden brown, about 35 minutes. Remove and let cool for 10 minutes. Garnish with the mint leaves before serving.

YIELD: **8 SERVINGS**

ACTIVE TIME: **10 MINUTES**

TOTAL TIME: **1 HOUR AND 30 MINUTES**

Pumpkin Quiche

INGREDIENTS

5 LARGE EGGS

1 CUP UNSWEETENED PUMPKIN PUREE

1 CUP CRÈME FRAÎCHE (SEE PAGE 199 FOR HOMEMADE)

½ CUP MILK

½ CUP HEAVY CREAM

1 CUP GRATED PARMESAN CHEESE, PLUS MORE FOR GARNISH

½ TEASPOON KOSHER SALT

½ TEASPOON BLACK PEPPER

1 PERFECT PIECRUST, BLIND BAKED (SEE PAGES 10–11)

⅓ CUP FRESH SAGE LEAVES, FINELY CHOPPED

DIRECTIONS

1. Preheat the oven to 350°F. Place the eggs, pumpkin puree, crème fraîche, milk, cream, Parmesan, salt, and pepper in a mixing bowl and stir to combine. Pour the mixture into the piecrust and gently shake the pie plate to distribute evenly. Sprinkle the sage leaves over the top.

2. Place the quiche in the oven and bake until it is puffy and golden brown, about 35 minutes. Remove and let cool for 10 minutes. Garnish with additional Parmesan before serving.

YIELD: **8 SERVINGS**

ACTIVE TIME: **25 MINUTES**

TOTAL TIME: **1 HOUR AND 45 MINUTES**

Sausage & Feta Quiche

INGREDIENTS

2 TABLESPOONS OLIVE OIL

½ LB. ITALIAN SAUSAGE, CHOPPED

¼ CUP DICED RED ONION

1 SMALL TOMATO, DICED

¼ CUP KALAMATA OLIVES, PITTED AND HALVED

2 CUPS SPINACH

4 EGGS

2 CUPS WHOLE MILK

1 TEASPOON KOSHER SALT

1 TEASPOON BLACK PEPPER

1 PERFECT PIECRUST, BLIND BAKED (SEE PAGES 10–11)

½ CUP CRUMBLED FETA CHEESE

DIRECTIONS

1. Preheat the oven to 350°F. Place the olive oil in a skillet and warm over medium heat. When the oil starts to shimmer, add the sausage and cook until it is browned all over, about 8 minutes. Transfer to a bowl, add the onion to the pan and cook until it starts to soften, about 5 minutes.

2. Add the tomato, olives, and spinach to the skillet and cook until the spinach wilts, about 2 minutes. Remove the pan from heat and allow the mixture to cool slightly.

3. Place the eggs in a bowl and beat until scrambled. Stir in the milk, salt, and pepper and set the mixture aside. Distribute the sausage and vegetable mixture over the piecrust, sprinkle the feta over the top, and then pour the egg mixture into the crust, shaking the pie plate to distribute evenly.

4. Place the quiche in the oven and bake for 35 minutes, until it is puffy and golden brown. Remove and let cool for 10 minutes before slicing and serving.

YIELD: **8 SERVINGS**

ACTIVE TIME: **25 MINUTES**

TOTAL TIME: **2 HOURS**

Spinach & Onion Quiche

INGREDIENTS

2 TABLESPOONS OLIVE OIL

1 RED ONION, SLICED

8 CUPS BABY SPINACH

1 PERFECT PIECRUST, BLIND BAKED (SEE PAGES 10–11)

6 LARGE EGGS

2 LARGE EGG YOLKS

1 CUP CRÈME FRAÎCHE (SEE PAGE 199 FOR HOMEMADE)

½ CUP MILK

½ CUP HEAVY CREAM

½ CUP GRATED GRUYÈRE CHEESE, PLUS MORE FOR GARNISH

¾ CUP GRATED PARMESAN CHEESE

¼ TEASPOON KOSHER SALT

¼ TEASPOON BLACK PEPPER

DIRECTIONS

1. Preheat the oven to 350°F. Place 1 tablespoon of the oil in a large skillet and warm over medium heat. When the oil starts to shimmer, add the onion and cook until it starts to soften, about 5 minutes. Transfer the onion to a paper towel–lined plate.

2. Place the remaining oil in the skillet, add the spinach, and cook until it starts to wilt, about 2 minutes. Transfer to a colander and press down on the spinach to remove as much water as possible from it. Distribute the onion and spinach in the piecrust.

3. Place the eggs, egg yolks, crème fraîche, milk, cream, cheeses, salt, and pepper in a mixing bowl and stir to combine. Pour the mixture into the piecrust and gently shake the pie plate to distribute evenly.

4. Place the quiche in the oven and bake until it is puffy and golden brown, about 35 minutes. Remove and let cool for 10 minutes. Garnish with additional Gruyère before serving.

YIELD: **8 SERVINGS**

ACTIVE TIME: **1 HOUR**

TOTAL TIME: **2 HOURS AND 45 MINUTES**

Chicken Pot Pies

INGREDIENTS

FOR THE FILLING

1½ LBS. CHICKEN BREASTS

3 TABLESPOONS OLIVE OIL

1 STICK UNSALTED BUTTER

2 CARROTS, PEELED AND DICED

3 CELERY TALKS, DICED

2 YELLOW ONIONS, DICED

5 CUPS CHICKEN STOCK

¾ CUP ALL-PURPOSE FLOUR

1 CUP FROZEN CORN

1 CUP FROZEN PEAS

FOR THE PIECRUSTS

5 CUPS ALL-PURPOSE FLOUR, PLUS MORE AS NEEDED

2½ TEASPOONS KOSHER SALT

1 TEASPOON BLACK PEPPER

2 TABLESPOONS FINELY CHOPPED FRESH PARSLEY

1 TABLESPOON FINELY CHOPPED FRESH THYME

4 STICKS UNSALTED BUTTER

1 CUP ICE-COLD WATER, PLUS 2 TEASPOONS

1 EGG YOLK

DIRECTIONS

1. Preheat the oven to 400°F. To begin preparations for the filling, place the chicken breasts in a baking dish and drizzle the olive oil over them. Place in the oven and bake until the internal temperature is 160°F, about 15 to 20 minutes. Remove and let cool. When cool enough to handle, cut the chicken into bite-sized cubes. Lower the oven temperature to 375°F.

2. Place the butter, carrots, celery, and onions in a large saucepan and cook over medium-high heat until the onions turn translucent, about 3 minutes. Place the stock in a separate saucepan and warm over medium-high heat.

3. Add the flour to the vegetable mixture and cook, while stirring constantly, until the mixture gives off a nutty aroma, about 2 minutes. Pour the warmed stock into the pan while stirring to prevent lumps from forming. When the stock has been incorporated and the mixture is smooth, add the chicken, corn, and peas. Cook for 2 minutes and then remove from heat.

4. To begin preparations for the piecrusts, place the flour, 2 teaspoons of the salt, the pepper, parsley, and thyme in a large mixing bowl and stir to combine. Divide the butter into tablespoons and place them in the freezer for 15 minutes. Place the flour mixture and the butter in a food processor and pulse 4 to 5 times. Slowly pour the 1 cup of ice-cold water into the food processor and pulse until the mixture is just combined. Transfer the dough to a flour-dusted work surface and knead until it is smooth. Place the dough in the refrigerator for at least 20 minutes.

Continued...

5. Remove the dough from the refrigerator and divide it into 16 pieces. Roll each piece to a thickness of ⅛ inch. Place one crust in eight different miniature cast-iron skillets or au gratin dishes, making sure that the crust extends over the sides. Prick each crust with a fork, cover with a piece of parchment paper, and fill with uncooked rice. Place in the oven and bake for 15 minutes. Remove, discard the rice, and fill each crust with some of the chicken-and-vegetable mixture.

6. Lay another crust over the top of each pie and crimp the edges to seal. Place the 2 teaspoons of water, egg yolk, and remaining salt in a bowl and beat to combine. Cut a slit in the top crust of each pie and brush with the egg wash. Place the pies on a baking sheet, place them in the oven, and bake until the top crusts are golden brown, 35 to 40 minutes. Remove from the oven and let cool slightly before serving.

YIELD: **6 SERVINGS**

ACTIVE TIME: **30 MINUTES**

TOTAL TIME: **1 HOUR AND 45 MINUTES**

Cottage Pie

INGREDIENTS

6 RUSSET POTATOES, PEELED AND CHOPPED

½ TEASPOON KOSHER SALT

1 STICK UNSALTED BUTTER, DIVIDED INTO TABLESPOONS

½ CUP MILK

¼ CUP PLAIN YOGURT

SALT AND PEPPER, TO TASTE

1 TABLESPOON OLIVE OIL

½ YELLOW ONION, MINCED

1 LB. GROUND BEEF

2 CUPS FROZEN PEAS

1 CUP CORN KERNELS

DIRECTIONS

1. Preheat the oven to 350°F. Place the potato pieces in a large saucepan and cover with cold water. Add the salt and bring the water to a boil. Reduce heat so that the water simmers and cook the potatoes until fork-tender, about 20 minutes.

2. Drain the potatoes and place them in a large bowl. Add 6 tablespoons of the butter, milk, and yogurt and mash until smooth. Season with salt and pepper and set aside.

3. Place a 12-inch cast-iron skillet over medium heat, add the olive oil, and cook the onion until it turns translucent, about 4 minutes. Add the ground beef and cook, while breaking it up with a fork, until browned, about 8 minutes. Drain the fat from the skillet, stir in the peas and corn, and season with salt and pepper.

4. Spread the mashed potatoes over the meat and vegetables, using a rubber spatula to smooth the top. Cut the remaining butter into slivers and dot the potatoes with them.

5. Cover the skillet with foil, place in the oven, and bake for 30 minutes. Remove the foil and bake for another 10 minutes, until the potatoes are starting to brown. Remove from the oven and let cool for 5 minutes before serving.

Mushroom & Chard Shepherd's Pie

YIELD: **4 TO 6 SERVINGS**

ACTIVE TIME: **30 MINUTES**

TOTAL TIME: **1 HOUR AND 45 MINUTES**

INGREDIENTS

6 RUSSET POTATOES, PEELED AND CHOPPED

½ TEASPOON KOSHER SALT, PLUS MORE TO TASTE

11 TABLESPOONS UNSALTED BUTTER, DIVIDED INTO INDIVIDUAL TABLESPOONS

½ CUP MILK

¼ CUP PLAIN YOGURT

BLACK PEPPER, TO TASTE

1 SMALL ONION, MINCED

3 CUPS CHOPPED MUSHROOMS

1 BUNCH SWISS CHARD, WASHED AND CHOPPED

1 TABLESPOON WORCESTERSHIRE SAUCE

OLIVE OIL, AS NEEDED

DIRECTIONS

1. Preheat the oven to 350°F. Place the potatoes in a large saucepan and cover with cold water. Add the salt. Bring the water to a boil, reduce to a simmer, and cook the potatoes until fork-tender, about 20 minutes.

2. Drain the potatoes and place them in a large bowl. Add 6 tablespoons of the butter, the milk, and the yogurt and mash the potatoes until they are smooth and creamy. Season with salt and pepper and set aside.

3. In a 12-inch cast-iron skillet, melt 3 tablespoons of the butter over medium heat. Add the onion and cook until translucent, about 3 minutes. Add the mushrooms, the chopped stems of the chard (not the leaves), and the Worcestershire sauce. Cook for about 4 minutes, while stirring frequently, then reduce the heat to low and continue to cook until the mushrooms and chard stems are soft, another 5 minutes. If the pan seems dry, add some olive oil.

4. Increase the heat to medium and add the chard leaves. Cook, while stirring constantly, until the leaves wilt, about 3 minutes. Remove the skillet from heat and season with salt and pepper.

5. Spread the mashed potatoes over the mixture, distributing the potatoes evenly and smoothing the top with a rubber spatula. Cut the remaining 2 tablespoons of butter into slivers and dot the potatoes with them.

6. Cover with foil and bake for 25 minutes. Remove the foil and bake for another 10 minutes, until the mashed potatoes are browned and the filling is bubbling. Remove and let cool briefly before serving.

YIELD: **8 SERVINGS**

ACTIVE TIME: **30 MINUTES**

TOTAL TIME: **1 HOUR AND 15 MINUTES**

Turkish Spinach Pie

INGREDIENTS

2 TABLESPOONS OLIVE OIL

1 YELLOW ONION, MINCED

¾ TEASPOON KOSHER SALT, PLUS MORE TO TASTE

3 GARLIC CLOVES, MINCED

8 CUPS FROZEN SPINACH, THAWED AND DRAINED

2 CUPS COTTAGE CHEESE, AT ROOM TEMPERATURE

1 CUP CRUMBLED FETA CHEESE

2 LARGE EGGS, LIGHTLY BEATEN

2 SCALLIONS, TRIMMED AND SLICED

¼ CUP FINELY CHOPPED FRESH PARSLEY

1 TABLESPOON FINELY CHOPPED FRESH DILL

½ TEASPOON BLACK PEPPER

PINCH OF GRATED FRESH NUTMEG

2 SHEETS OF FILO DOUGH

4 TABLESPOONS UNSALTED BUTTER, MELTED

DIRECTIONS

1. Preheat the oven to 350°F. Place the olive oil in a large skillet and warm over medium heat. When the oil starts to shimmer, add the onion and a pinch of salt and cook until the onion turns translucent, about 3 minutes. Stir in the garlic and cook until it just starts to brown, about 2 minutes. Remove the pan from heat and set it aside.

2. Place the spinach in a colander and press down to remove as much water from it as possible. Spread the spinach on paper towels, blot it dry, and chop. Add the chopped spinach to the skillet and cook over medium heat until all of the liquid has evaporated, about 3 minutes. Remove the pan from heat and set aside.

3. Place the cottage cheese, feta cheese, eggs, scallions, parsley, dill, pepper, nutmeg, and salt in a mixing bowl and stir to combine. Place the mixture in an 8-inch square baking dish, top with the spinach mixture, and then place a sheet of filo dough on top. Generously brush the filo with some of the melted butter, place the remaining sheet of filo on top, and brush with the remaining butter.

4. Place the pie in the oven and bake for about 35 minutes, until golden brown and crispy on top. Remove from the oven and let stand for 5 minutes before serving.

YIELD: **8 SERVINGS**

ACTIVE TIME: **25 MINUTES**

TOTAL TIME: **2 HOURS**

Tamale Pie

INGREDIENTS

FOR THE FILLING

3 CUPS GROUND BEEF

1 WHITE ONION, DICED

1 LARGE GREEN BELL PEPPER, STEMMED, SEEDED, AND DICED

½ TEASPOON KOSHER SALT, PLUS MORE TO TASTE

2 CUPS TOMATO SAUCE

1 (28 OZ.) CAN OF DICED TOMATOES

2 CUPS CORN KERNELS

¾ CUP SLICED BLACK OLIVES

2 GARLIC CLOVES, DICED

½ TABLESPOON SUGAR

2 TEASPOONS CUMIN

2 TEASPOONS CHILI POWDER

1 TEASPOON DRIED OREGANO

½ TEASPOON BLACK PEPPER

½ CUP SHREDDED MEXICAN CHEESE BLEND

Continued...

DIRECTIONS

1. To begin preparations for the filling, warm a Dutch oven over medium heat. Add the beef and cook, while breaking it up with a fork, until browned, about 8 minutes. Stir in the onion, green pepper, and a pinch of salt and cook until the vegetables have started to soften, about 5 minutes.

2. Drain the fat from the mixture, stir in the tomato sauce, diced tomatoes, corn, olives, garlic, sugar, cumin, chili powder, oregano, salt, and pepper. Bring to a simmer and cook, stirring occasionally, until the mixture thickens slightly, about 20 minutes. Remove from heat and stir in the cheese.

3. Preheat the oven to 375°F. To prepare the topping, place the cornmeal, salt, chili powder, and water in a saucepan and cook over medium heat until the mixture has thickened, about 15 minutes. Remove from heat, stir in the butter and cheese, and then spread the mixture in an even layer on top of the beef mixture.

4. Place the Dutch oven in the oven and bake until the topping has browned and is dry to the touch, about 45 minutes. Remove from the oven and let cool for 5 minutes before serving.

FOR THE TOPPING

1 CUP CORNMEAL

¾ TEASPOON KOSHER SALT

½ TEASPOON CHILI POWDER

2¾ CUPS WATER

1 TABLESPOON UNSALTED BUTTER

½ CUP SHREDDED MEXICAN CHEESE BLEND

YIELD: **6 SERVINGS**

ACTIVE TIME: **45 MINUTES**

TOTAL TIME: **3 HOURS AND 45 MINUTES**

Beef & Guinness Pie

INGREDIENTS

¼ CUP OLIVE OIL, PLUS 2 TABLESPOONS

2½ LBS. CHUCK STEAK, TRIMMED AND DICED

SALT AND PEPPER, TO TASTE

2 ONIONS, CHOPPED

2 CARROTS, PEELED AND CHOPPED

2 TABLESPOONS ALL-PURPOSE FLOUR, PLUS MORE AS NEEDED

1 TABLESPOON FINELY CHOPPED FRESH THYME

2 CUPS GUINNESS

1 (14 OZ.) CAN OF DICED TOMATOES

1 SHEET OF FROZEN PUFF PASTRY, THAWED

1 LARGE EGG, BEATEN

DIRECTIONS

1. Place the ¼ cup oil in a Dutch oven and warm over medium heat. When the oil starts to shimmer, season the beef with salt and pepper. Working in batches, add the beef to the pot and cook until it is browned all over. Transfer the browned beef to a plate and set aside.

2. Add the remaining oil and the onions to the pot and cook until they start to soften, about 5 minutes. While the onions are cooking, use a wooden spoon to scrape up any browned bits from the bottom of the Dutch oven. Add the carrots and cook for 2 minutes. Place the beef and its juices in the pot, sprinkle the flour on top, and cook, stirring constantly, for 2 minutes.

3. Add the thyme, Guinness, and tomatoes and season generously with salt and pepper. Bring to a boil and then reduce the heat so that the mixture simmers. Simmer until the beef is very tender, stirring occasionally, about 2½ hours. Remove from heat and let cool slightly.

4. Preheat the oven to 400°F. Place the sheet of puff pastry on a flour-dusted work surface and roll it out into a ¼-inch-thick circle. Place the beef mixture in a baking dish, place the pastry on top, and trim any excess. Brush the pastry with the egg and cut a few slits in the center.

5. Place in the oven and bake for about 30 minutes, until the pastry is crisp, puffy, and golden brown. Remove from the oven and let cool for 5 minutes before serving.

YIELD: **8 SERVINGS**

ACTIVE TIME: **30 MINUTES**

TOTAL TIME: **1 HOUR AND 45 MINUTES**

Tourtiere

INGREDIENTS

½ TEASPOON KOSHER SALT, PLUS MORE TO TASTE

2 LARGE RED SKIN POTATOES, PEELED AND CHOPPED

1 LB. GROUND PORK

1 LB. GROUND BEEF

1 SMALL ONION, MINCED

1 GARLIC CLOVE, MINCED

1 TEASPOON POULTRY SEASONING

½ TEASPOON CINNAMON

¼ TEASPOON GROUND CLOVES

¼ TEASPOON BLACK PEPPER

2 PERFECT PIECRUSTS (SEE PAGE 10)

1 LARGE EGG

1 TABLESPOON WATER

DIRECTIONS

1. Bring salted water to a boil in a large saucepan. Add the potatoes and cook until fork-tender, 15 to 18 minutes. Drain the potatoes, making sure to reserve ½ cup of the cooking water, and let them cool briefly.

2. While the potatoes are cooking, place the ground pork and ground beef in a Dutch oven and cook over medium heat, while breaking them up with a fork, until browned, about 8 minutes. Stir in the onion and garlic and cook until the onion starts to soften, about 5 minutes. Add the poultry seasoning, cinnamon, cloves, salt, and pepper, stir to incorporate, and remove the pan from heat.

3. Mash the potatoes until smooth. Stir the cooking water into the ground meat mixture and cook over medium heat until all of the liquid has been absorbed, 8 to 10 minutes. Remove from heat and stir in the mashed potatoes.

4. Preheat the oven to 425°F. Grease a 9-inch pie plate with nonstick cooking spray and place one of the crusts in it. Evenly distribute the meat-and-potato mixture in the crust, place the other crust over the top, and crimp the edge to seal. Combine the egg and water in a small bowl, brush the top crust with the egg wash, and cut four or five slits in it.

5. Place the pie in the oven and bake for about 45 minutes, until the top crust is golden brown and the filling is bubbling. Remove from the oven and briefly let cool before serving.

Chicken Bastilla

YIELD: **8 SERVINGS**

ACTIVE TIME: **45 MINUTES**

TOTAL TIME: **1 HOUR AND 30 MINUTES**

INGREDIENTS

2 TABLESPOONS OLIVE OIL, PLUS MORE AS NEEDED

3 CUPS GROUND CHICKEN

SALT AND PEPPER, TO TASTE

1 TABLESPOON UNSALTED BUTTER

1 YELLOW ONION, MINCED

2 GARLIC CLOVES, MINCED

1 TEASPOON GROUND GINGER

½ TEASPOON CINNAMON

¾ TEASPOON TURMERIC

PINCH OF SAFFRON

2½ CUPS CHICKEN STOCK

4 LARGE EGGS, BEATEN

⅔ CUP ALMOND MEAL

1 TEASPOON ORANGE BLOSSOM WATER

1 TEASPOON ORANGE ZEST

½ CUP FINELY CHOPPED FRESH PARSLEY, PLUS MORE FOR GARNISH

6 LARGE SHEETS OF FILO DOUGH

DIRECTIONS

1. Place the oil in a Dutch oven and warm over medium heat. When the oil starts to shimmer, add the ground chicken, season with salt, and cook, while using a fork to break it up, until it is browned, about 8 minutes. Transfer the chicken to a bowl and set aside.

2. Add the butter to the Dutch oven. When it has melted, add the onion and cook until it starts to soften, about 5 minutes. Add the garlic and spices and cook, stirring constantly, for 2 minutes. Return the chicken to the pot and pour in the chicken stock. Bring to a simmer and cook for 10 minutes, stirring occasionally.

3. Using a slotted spoon, transfer the chicken to a bowl. Raise the heat to medium-high and cook until the liquid has been reduced by half. Reduce the heat to low, stir in the eggs, and cook until the eggs are set, 2 to 3 minutes. Remove from heat, season with salt and pepper, and stir in the almond meal, orange blossom water, orange zest, and parsley.

4. Preheat the oven to 350°F. Brush a sheet of filo with olive oil and place it in a 9-inch pie plate. Place another sheet of filo on top and brush it with more olive oil. Evenly distribute the egg mixture on top, fold any excess filo over the mixture, and cover with another sheet of filo. Brush with olive oil, top with another sheet of filo, and brush it with more olive oil.

5. Evenly distribute the chicken on top, cover with the two remaining sheets of filo, and trim away any excess. Brush the filo with olive oil, place the pie in the oven, and bake for about 30 minutes, until it is crisp and golden brown. Remove from the oven and let cool for 5 minutes. Garnish with additional parsley before serving.

YIELD: **6 SERVINGS**

ACTIVE TIME: **35 MINUTES**

TOTAL TIME: **2 HOURS**

Fish Pie

INGREDIENTS

FOR THE TOPPING

1 TEASPOON KOSHER SALT, PLUS MORE TO TASTE

9 RUSSET POTATOES, PEELED AND DICED

1 STICK UNSALTED BUTTER, AT ROOM TEMPERATURE

½ CUP WHOLE MILK, WARMED

2 EGG YOLKS

¼ TEASPOON BLACK PEPPER

FOR THE FILLING

1 TABLESPOON OLIVE OIL

1 LEEK, SLICED AND RINSED WELL

4 TABLESPOONS UNSALTED BUTTER

¼ CUP ALL-PURPOSE FLOUR

2½ CUPS WHOLE MILK

½ CUP HEAVY CREAM

½ LB. BONELESS, SKINLESS HADDOCK FILLET, CHOPPED

½ LB. BONELESS, SKINLESS SALMON FILLET, CHOPPED

2 TABLESPOONS FINELY CHOPPED FRESH DILL, PLUS MORE FOR GARNISH

1 TEASPOON KOSHER SALT

½ TEASPOON BLACK PEPPER

DIRECTIONS

1. To prepare the topping, bring salted water to a boil in a large saucepan. Add the potatoes and cook until fork-tender, about 20 minutes. Drain, return them to the saucepan, and cook over medium-low heat until they are dry, about 2 minutes. Add the butter and mash to incorporate. Add the remaining ingredients and mash until smooth. Place the mashed potatoes in a large piping bag fitted with a star-shaped tip and set aside.

2. Preheat the oven to 350°F. To begin preparations for the filling, place the olive oil in a skillet and warm over medium heat. When the oil starts to shimmer, add the leek and cook until it is soft, about 10 minutes. Remove the pan from heat.

3. Place the butter in a large saucepan and melt over medium heat. Add the flour and cook, stirring constantly, until the mixture turns golden brown, 2 to 3 minutes. Gradually incorporate the milk and cream and bring the mixture to a simmer. Cook for 8 to 10 minutes, stirring frequently. Fold in the fish and leek and then stir in the dill, salt, and pepper. Transfer the mixture to a rectangular baking dish.

4. Pipe rows of the topping over the filling, place the pie in the oven, and bake for about 45 minutes, until the top is golden brown. Remove from the oven, let cool for 5 minutes, and garnish with additional dill before serving.

YIELD: **8 SERVINGS**

ACTIVE TIME: **40 MINUTES**

TOTAL TIME: **1 HOUR AND 30 MINUTES**

Lamb Pie

INGREDIENTS

¼ CUP OLIVE OIL

3 CUPS GROUND LAMB

½ ONION, MINCED

½ LEEK, SLICED AND RINSED WELL

2 GARLIC CLOVES, MINCED

2 TEASPOONS CUMIN

1 TEASPOON CORIANDER

1½ TEASPOONS CINNAMON

½ TEASPOON PAPRIKA

½ CUP CHICKEN STOCK

2 TEASPOONS HONEY

¼ CUP FINELY CHOPPED FRESH PARSLEY

1 TABLESPOON FINELY CHOPPED FRESH THYME

½ CUP CASHEWS

1 TEASPOON KOSHER SALT

½ TEASPOON BLACK PEPPER

6 SHEETS OF FILO DOUGH

1 TABLESPOON CONFECTIONERS' SUGAR

DIRECTIONS

1. Place 2 tablespoons of the olive oil in a Dutch oven and warm over medium heat. When the oil starts to shimmer, add the lamb and cook, while breaking it up with a fork, until it is browned, about 8 minutes. Stir in the onion, leek, and garlic and cook over medium heat until the onion and leek have started to soften, about 5 minutes.

2. Stir in the cumin, coriander, ½ teaspoon of the cinnamon, and the paprika and cook for 2 minutes. Add the stock, honey, parsley, thyme, cashews, salt, and pepper, stir to combine, and bring to a boil. Cook until almost all of the liquid has evaporated, 1 to 2 minutes. Remove from heat and set aside.

3. Preheat the oven to 400°F. Brush a sheet of filo with some of the remaining olive oil and place it in a 9-inch pie plate. Place another sheet of filo on top and brush it with more of the olive oil. Repeat with another sheet of filo. Evenly distribute the lamb mixture on top, fold any excess filo over the mixture, and cover with another sheet of filo. Brush with olive oil and then cover it with another sheet of filo. Brush this with olive oil, place the remaining sheet on top, and tuck the filo in around the filling.

4. Brush the top of the pie with olive oil, place it in the oven, and bake for about 35 minutes, until golden brown on top. Remove from the oven and let cool for 15 minutes. Sprinkle the confectioners' sugar and cinnamon on top before serving.

YIELD: **4 SERVINGS**

ACTIVE TIME: **30 MINUTES**

TOTAL TIME: **1 HOUR AND 30 MINUTES**

Tartiflette Pie

INGREDIENTS

1 SHEET OF FROZEN PUFF PASTRY, THAWED

ALL-PURPOSE FLOUR, AS NEEDED

SALT AND PEPPER, TO TASTE

8 FINGERLING POTATOES

2 TABLESPOONS UNSALTED BUTTER

1 YELLOW ONION, SLICED THIN

1 CUP PANCETTA LARDONS

⅔ CUP DRY WHITE WINE

¾ CUP HEAVY CREAM

1 SMALL WHEEL REBLOCHON CHEESE, CHOPPED

⅓ CUP SLIVERED ALMONDS, TOASTED

2 TABLESPOONS FINELY CHOPPED FRESH PARSLEY

1 LARGE EGG

1 TABLESPOON WATER

DIRECTIONS

1. Cut the sheet of puff pastry into two pieces. Place one piece on a flour-dusted work surface and roll it into a 9- to 10-inch circle that is approximately ¼ inch thick. Place the pastry in a greased 9-inch pie plate, trim any excess, prick the pastry with a fork, and refrigerate. Envelop the remaining piece of pastry in plastic wrap and refrigerate it as well.

2. Bring salted water to a boil in a large saucepan. Add the potatoes and cook until fork-tender, about 20 minutes. Drain the potatoes and let them cool for a few minutes. When cool enough to handle, chop them.

3. While the potatoes are cooking, place 1 tablespoon of the butter in a saucepan and melt it over medium heat. Add the onion and pancetta and cook until they begin to brown, about 8 minutes. Add the wine, bring the mixture to a boil, and cook until almost all of the wine has evaporated. Add the cream and cook until it has reduced by one-third. Remove the saucepan from heat and set aside.

4. Place the remaining butter in a large skillet and melt over medium heat. Add the potatoes and a pinch of salt and pepper and sauté until the potatoes are golden brown, about 6 to 8 minutes. Stir the potatoes and the Reblochon into the creamy pancetta-and-onion mixture. Stir in the almonds and parsley, season with salt and pepper, and let the mixture cool slightly. Remove the pastry-lined pie plate and the piece of wrapped pastry from the refrigerator and let them come to room temperature.

Continued...

5. Place the piece of pastry on a flour-dusted work surface and roll it out into a 9- to 10-inch round. Spoon the filling into the pie plate, place the pastry on top, and trim away any excess. Place the egg and water in a small bowl and stir to combine. Brush the top crust with the egg wash and poke four or five slits in the center.

6. Place the pie in the oven and bake for about 30 minutes, until it is puffy and golden brown. Remove from the oven and let cool for 10 minutes before serving.

YIELD: **8 SERVINGS**

ACTIVE TIME: **15 MINUTES**

TOTAL TIME: **5 HOURS**

Tomato Pie

INGREDIENTS

⅔ CUP MILK

½ CUP FINELY CHOPPED FRESH ROSEMARY, PLUS MORE FOR GARNISH

3 CUPS CREAM CHEESE, AT ROOM TEMPERATURE

1 CUP GRATED PARMESAN CHEESE

½ TEASPOON KOSHER SALT

¼ TEASPOON BLACK PEPPER, PLUS MORE TO TASTE

1 PERFECT PIECRUST, BLIND BAKED (SEE PAGES 10–11)

4 TO 5 LARGE HEIRLOOM TOMATOES, CORED AND SLICED

1 TEASPOON DRIED OREGANO

DIRECTIONS

1. Place the milk and rosemary in a small saucepan and warm over low heat for 3 to 4 minutes. Strain into a mixing bowl, add the cream cheese, ¾ cup of the Parmesan, the salt, and pepper and beat with a handheld mixer until smooth. Evenly distribute the mixture in the piecrust. Cover with plastic wrap and refrigerate for 4 hours.

2. Remove the pie from the refrigerator and arrange the slices of tomato on top. Sprinkle the remaining Parmesan and the oregano over the pie, and garnish with additional rosemary.

Beet & Goat Cheese Pie

YIELD: **8 SERVINGS**

ACTIVE TIME: **15 MINUTES**

TOTAL TIME: **5 HOURS**

INGREDIENTS

⅔ CUP MILK

½ CUP FINELY CHOPPED FRESH ROSEMARY

2 CUPS GOAT CHEESE, AT ROOM TEMPERATURE

1 CUP CREAM CHEESE, AT ROOM TEMPERATURE

½ CUP GRATED PARMESAN CHEESE

½ TEASPOON KOSHER SALT

¼ TEASPOON BLACK PEPPER

1 PERFECT PIECRUST, BLIND BAKED (SEE PAGES 10–11)

2 LARGE BEETS, SCRUBBED

½ CUP PINE NUTS, LIGHTLY TOASTED

1 TABLESPOON BALSAMIC GLAZE, FOR GARNISH

½ CUP BEET GREENS, FOR GARNISH (OPTIONAL)

DIRECTIONS

1. Place the milk and rosemary in a small saucepan and warm over low heat for 3 to 4 minutes. Strain into a mixing bowl, add the goat cheese, cream cheese, Parmesan, salt, and pepper and beat with a handheld mixer until smooth. Evenly distribute the mixture in the blind-baked crust. Cover with plastic wrap and refrigerate for 4 hours.

2. Preheat the oven to 400°F. Wrap the beets in aluminum foil and place them on a baking sheet. Place them in the oven and roast for about 1 hour, until fork-tender. Remove from the oven and let cool. When the beets are cool enough to handle, peel them and then slice them thin.

3. Remove the pie from the refrigerator and arrange the slices of beet on top. Garnish with the pine nuts, balsamic glaze, and, if using, the beet greens.

METRIC CONVERSIONS

U.S. Measurement	Approximate Metric Liquid Measurement	Approximate Metric Dry Measurement
1 teaspoon	5 ml	5 g
1 tablespoon or ½ ounce	15 ml	14 g
1 ounce or ⅛ cup	30 ml	29 g
¼ cup or 2 ounces	60 ml	57 g
⅓ cup	80 ml	76 g
½ cup or 4 ounces	120 ml	113 g
⅔ cup	160 ml	151 g
¾ cup or 6 ounces	180 ml	170 g
1 cup or 8 ounces or ½ pint	240 ml	227 g
1½ cups or 12 ounces	350 ml	340 g
2 cups or 1 pint or 16 ounces	475 ml	454 g
3 cups or 1½ pints	700 ml	680 g
4 cups or 2 pints or 1 quart	950 ml	908 g

INDEX

D

E

F

G

H

I

K

L

M

N

O

P

Q

R

S

T

V

W

Y

Z

ABOUT CIDER MILL PRESS BOOK PUBLISHERS

❋ ❋ ❋

Good ideas ripen with time. From seed to harvest, Cider Mill Press brings fine reading, information, and entertainment together between the covers of its creatively crafted books. Our Cider Mill bears fruit twice a year, publishing a new crop of titles each spring and fall.

CIDER MILL PRESS
BOOK PUBLISHERS

"Where Good Books Are Ready for Press"

501 Nelson Place
Nashville, Tennessee 37214

cidermillpress.com